Ludonarrative Sy

Lyz Reblin-Renshaw

Ludonarrative Synchronicity in the 'BioShock' Trilogy

palgrave
macmillan

Lyz Reblin-Renshaw
Independent Scholar
Tujunga, CA, USA

ISBN 978-3-030-63867-2 ISBN 978-3-030-63868-9 (eBook)
https://doi.org/10.1007/978-3-030-63868-9

This Palgrave Pivot imprint is published by the registered company Springer Nature Switzerland AG.
The registered company address is: Gewerbestrasse 11, 6330 Cham, Switzerland

Acknowledgments

Thirteen years ago, sitting in a dimly lit dorm room at Chapman University, I never would have thought that the game I was watching be played would lead me to this point. There are so many people I wish to thank for helping me turn a hobby into legitime research.

To my Mom for being willing to overlook the M rating on violent video games when I was younger and to my Dad for not returning said games after seeing me playing them, laughing with glee.

To my advisors: Carlos Amador, John Blood, Adam Crowley, Stefka Hristova, Diane Shoos, and Sharon Strover. You pushed me to what I thought were my limits and beyond.

To my students (especially the Madi's), willing to be my guinea pigs as I tested out the material for classroom suitability.

To Alex: the Luigi to my Mario, the Ken to my Ryu, my eternal Player Two. Thank you for always reminding me which button was crouch.

And most importantly to the baristas at Bookworm in Houghton, K.C. Bonker's in Hancock, and Starbucks at Foothill & Willalee. You are the real heroes to us scholars.

Contents

CHAPTER 1

Introduction

Abstract The introduction covers the manuscript's core methodology, ludonarrative synchronicity, the history behind the narrative/gameplay debate, and the relevance of the *BioShock* trilogy to the focus on player choice and control.

Keywords Ludonarrative synchronicity • Ken Levine • Mechanics • Dynamics • Affect • Narrative

When *BioShock* was released in 2007, it was not the best-selling first-person shooter (FPS) game of its day. *Call of Duty 4: Modern Warfare* on PC outsold the Irrational Game title, along with both *Call of Duty 4* and *Halo 3* on the Xbox 360. *BioShock* did not even make the top ten best sellers for the PlayStation 3 that year.[1]

However, in relation to artistic credibility, *BioShock* was the talk of the town. *Gamespy* wrote "it is a foregone conclusion that you will buy this game and love it… put simply, *BioShock* is an unparalleled achievement. No other game comes even remotely close to it in terms of raw emotional connection."[2] *XBOX 360* review was nothing short of eurphoric, stating that "There's such a wit in the writing, such an understanding of people that the lines approach the heights of classical aphorisms, great quotable sayings that match the best products of the minds of antiquity. This sounds

L. Reblin-Renshaw, *Ludonarrative Synchronicity in the 'BioShock' Trilogy*, https://doi.org/10.1007/978-3-030-63868-9_1

like ridiculous overblown hyperbole, but it isn't."[3] Even non-traditional gaming review sources lauded the game. The *New York Times* declared that "anchored by its provocative, morality-based story line, sumptuous art direction and superb voice acting, *BioShock* can also hold its head high among the best games ever made."[4] Writing for the *Los Angeles Times*, Pete Metzger continued the high praise:

> A game like *BioShock*… changes everything. Sure, it's fun to play, looks spectacular and is easy to control. But it also does something no other game has done to date: It really makes you feel. After all, aren't video games supposed to make us lose ourselves in vast imaginary worlds? *BioShock* does. And more.[5]

It is arguable whether the purpose of video games is purely immersion, but active interactivity was the stated goal of *BioShock*. Ken Levine, creator of the franchise, wanted to build a game in which the "players were not an observer of narrative, but a participant."[6] In order to achieve this, he needed to find a way to grant players a sense of agency and control beyond what had been done with previous first-person shooters. Seb Franklin, in his chapter "From Narrated Subjects to Programmable Objects" featured in *Control: Digitality as Cultural Logic*, argues that true control is in the hand of the programmers and the strength of their power is in their ability to maintain this trickery through veiled subterfuge. Rather than attempting to hide these outside forces at play, Levine chose to expose them. *BioShock*, and its two follow-ups, is a postmodern exploration of agency, simultaneously critiquing how players interact with and are affected by video games, but also falls prey to the very critiques it illuminates. These moments, when the player realizes their passivity, their inability to fully control the game's narrative, that their choices do not matter, are failures to retain ludonarrative synchronicity. This term of my creation refers to moments when the ludological components of a video game align with the narrative elements at play. In the case of *BioShock*, when they desynchronize, active interactivity by means of control and choice faulters. It is through this framework that I intend to analyze how Ken Levine tried to build the impossible, emerging players in a virtual reality of their own creation.

TUTORIAL

Defining terms is tricky. There is an unspoken assumption behind the practice: that if a definition is correct-if it manages to capture the essence of the thing under discussion-then everything that logically follows from that definition will be correct too. And so scholars often take great pains to demonstrate that there is a strong correlation between their definitions and reality.

The "correction" of a definition isn't a property of the relationship between the word and reality; it is a function of the conversation that the definition facilitates. And, indeed, multiple contradictory definitions can all be equally "correct" if they each manage to independently structure a producing discourse.[7]

Before exploring in detail how I will undertake such an analysis, it is imperative to establish an overview of previous writings about narratological studies, ludology, and their interaction to better contextualize where my research differs.

Gameplay

In the debut issue of *Game Studies*, the first academic, peer-reviewed journal dedicated to the field, editor-in-chief Espen Aarseth declared the year 2001 "Year One of *Computer Game Studies* as an emerging, viable, international, academic field."[8] Along with the premiere of the journal, 2001 also featured the first international scholarly conference focusing on computer games and it witnessed the rise of game studies as a serious field of study in academia.

Another cause for Aarseth's proclamation was work performed by his colleague at the IT University of Copenhagen, Gonzalo Frasca, who is attributed with coining the usage of the term "ludology" in 1999.[9] Frasca defines ludology as the "discipline that studies game and play activities."[10] His term shares a history with earlier non-video game ludic studies. Frasca refers to grammarian A. S. Hornby, child psychologist Jean Piaget, anthropologist Daniel Vidart, and philosopher Andre Lalande, all as scholars who separated the functions of "game" and "play." It was sociologist Roger Caillois who sought to find a balance between use of the word *paidia* (playfulness) and ludus (formal rule-based game behavior). In *Man, Play, and Games* (1961), Caillois proposed analyzing games as part of a spectrum that lay between play and logic.

In this analysis, I rely on the definition of gameplay established by Robin Hunicke, Marc LeBlanc, & Robert Zubek and their concept of MDA (mechanics-dynamics-aesthetics). Their lecture series, "MDA: A formal approach to game design and game research," presented over several years at the Games Developer Conference was intended to establish a methodology to be shared by scholars and developers alike and their terminology has since become industry standard.[11] For Hunicke, LeBlanc and Zubek, gameplay consists of mechanics, dynamics, and aesthetics.

Mechanics

Mechanics are the ludus of a game, that is the rules at play. They refer to all necessary pieces that one needs to play the game, including the equipment, the venue, or anything else necessary for play to be had. In considering the game as a system, the mechanics are the complete description of that system. Another way to consider mechanics is as a "system of constraints".[12] Designer and scholar Brian Upton, building upon the work of academics Katie Salen and Eric Zimmerman, explains that the rules of a game (not just video games) are a system of constraints, a varied group that can include:

> the physical geometry of a level, or the behavior of the enemy AI, or the amount of damage that a hand grenade does… Anything in the game that proscribes the player's actions is a constraint. The player is free to move around within the game world, to trigger actions, even to change the world's configuration, but always within limits laid down by the game itself.[13]

But mechanics do not need to be constraining. For instance, a game like *Borderlands* (2009), a bizarro sci-fi FPS set on the perilous planet Pandora, is filled with kooky characters, and even crazier physics. In the game, players take control of a Vault Hunter, inter-planetary mercenaries with little regards to the rules or laws. As such, the laws of physics in the game are nigh non-existent.[14] When a player falls from a great height, despite the hard impact, there is no loss of health. The lack of damage, a cartoonish effect in a game filled with outlandish aesthetics, is a mechanic that reflects the topsy-turvy tone of the game.

Dynamics

Dynamics refers to the "behavior" of the game, the actual events and phenomena that occur as the game is played. When viewing the game in terms of its dynamics, the question asked is, "What happens when the game is played?" The relationship between dynamics and mechanics is one of emergence. A game's dynamics emerge from its mechanics.[15] If the mechanics are a set of rules or a system of constraints, then dynamics are *how* players operate within that system. When playing *Dishonored* (2012), a first-person stealth action-adventure game where the player undertakes the role of a scorned assassin Corvo, choosing to sneak past a guard rather than execute him is an example of the game's dynamics. A dynamic choice need not be a decision between a better or worse action, though the outcomes they produce may differ. If the player executes a guard, then his comrades might hear the struggle and be alerted to Corvo's presence. If the player fails to properly perform a stealth move, which is more difficult than most execution mechanics, then they might lose more health in the process. Choosing stealth over vicious is not a right or wrong choice, but purely a matter of a gamer's desired play style.

Aesthetics/Affects

In Hunicke, eBlanc, and Zubek's initial proposal of MDA as a formal analysis of gameplay, the A stood for "aesthetics." Aesthetics, in MDA, is similar to the concept of *paidia* discussed by Calios, the desirable emotional responses we have when we play. A game's aesthetics emerge from its dynamics; how the game behaves determines how it makes the player feel.[16] Another way of looking at aesthetics, according to Dartmouth's Mary Flanagan and NYU's Helen Nissenbaum is that they instill a value for the player, whether it is a sense of control, competition, satisfaction, or reward.[17]

I find the term "aesthetics" problematic. Traditionally, aesthetics has been defined broadly as having "everything that to do with works of art or with the sense of beauty."[18] This, however, doesn't capture how crucial the relationship between mechanics and dynamics is to produce a structure of feeling. That is why I have chosen to maintain the MDA acronym by using the term "affect," rather than aesthetic.

Affect, as used in the field of cultural studies, is more than just a sensation, emotion, and feeling. Gregory Seigworth and Melissa Gregg, in their seminal collection *The Affect Theory Reader*, argue that affect "at its most anthropomorphic, is the name given to those forces-visceral forces beneath, alongside or generally other than conscious knowing, vital forces insisting beyond emotion-that can serve to drive us toward movement, toward thought".[19] A video game's affects are its emotional content, the desirable emotional responses that players have that result from playing the game. A game's affects emerge from its dynamics[20]; how the game behaves determines how it makes the player feel. For instance, the difference in affect between two racing games from 1997, *Mario Kart 64* and *Diddy Kong Racing*, is that the former intends to be fun with its random item generator mechanics and its lack of dynamic options to compensate for this apparent chaos. *Diddy Kong Racing*, on the other hand, has much more strategic dynamic capabilities due to its hierarchical item generator system, thus creating a more competitive affect.

For Stuart Hall disciple Lawrence Grossberg, affect is "the gap between meaningful and knowable, but nevertheless livable" or in this case playable.[21] This is why it is important to distinguish between intention or assumed affect and affect as played. Just because the developer's aim to have a specific affect with their game, does not mean their intention will be matched when players experience the game. Using another Nintendo product as an example, series director Masahiror Sakurai designed *Smash Bros. Melee* (2001) to be for casual players, going as far to say that those playing the game competitively were "playing the game wrong."[22] However, the *Super Smash Bros.* franchise has now become one of the most popular competitive fighting game series on the scene. The game's affect, in this case, is competitive, not "fun and interesting" like Sakurai wanted.[23]

Genre

Whereas narrative tropes such as character archetypes, setting, and plot are the base for most literary and cinematic genres, gameplay defines a video game's genre. This analysis will be adhering to Mark J. P. Wolf, who argues "player participation is arguably the central determinant in describing and classifying video games, more so even than iconography."[24] Mark J. P. Wolf argues that "player participation is arguably the central determinant in describing and classifying video games, more so even than iconography"[25] For instance, a game like *Super Mario Bros.* (1985), in which players direct Mario to jump from platform to platform, beam to beam, cloud to cloud, is a "platformer." A role-playing game (RPGs) such as *Dragon Age: Inquisition* (2014), centers on the player creating his character whether it is by the avatar's appearance, skills, or social interactions.

BioShock is an example of a first-person shooter (FPS), a game where the player controls the character via the eyes of the avatar, shooting down enemies. According to Janet Murray, in her seminal piece *Hamlet on the*

Holodeck, "an avatar is a graphical figure like a character in a video game".[26] And in a FPS video game like *BioShock*, disembodied hands, wrist, and forearms typically are the only portions of the player's avatar presented on screen. For a first-person shooter there are two aspects that separate these games from other genres.

The first is the game's use of a first-person camera. Using the terminology first-person "point of view" is a matter of contention, best explored by Alexander Galloway in his essay "Origins of the First-Person Shooter." This essay appeared in his collection *Gaming: Essays on Algorithmic Culture* which was meant to "formulate a few conceptual movements, a few conceptual algorithms, for thinking about video games… [but] above all, this book is about loving video games".[27] In his "Origins of the First-Person Shooter," Alexander Galloway compares the subjective camera shot of film noir to the first-person point of view camera in FPS. For Galloway, a subjective shot is one of accuracy "when the camera shows what the actual eyes of a character would see", while a POV shot is a generalized approximation.[28] This goes against visual studies scholar Frederic Jameson who describes "'Point of view' in the strictest sense of seeing through a character's eyes".[29] Galloway clarifies his claim by noting that "subjective shots are more extreme in their physiological mimicking of actual vision, for, as stated, they pretend to peer outward from the eyes of an actual character rather than simply to approximate a similar line of sight".[30] He explicates himself from this argument of terms by saying that "video games are the first mass media to effectively employ the first-person subjective perspective… used to achieve an intuitive sense of affective motion.[31] Rather than ask if modern-day FPS feature subjective or POV shots, he emphasizes what these shots create: action? I emphasize modern-day as the graphic capabilities of early FPS such as *Doom* and *Wolfenstein* wouldn't allow for loose, natural camera movements. Nowadays, with better technology, some FPS can mimic the physiological state of a character, such as blurring one's vision after being injured or near death. As for why I choose to use the term "camera" rather than either point of view or subjective view, "camera" emphasizes the player's control over their gaze. They are moving the camera, it is the player's viewpoint, not their avatar's.

The second integral aspect of FPS as a genre is the shooting mechanic. Continuing with Galloway's essay, weapons are as equally essential to the FPS as the subjective perspective, with how an avatar's weapon appears on screen.[32] However, Galloway does not see violence as a key for these types of games. FPSs are not the only video game genre that feature violence.

He argues that even a game like *Metal Gear Solid* (1998) or *Thief* (2014) that feature weapons and killing, emphasize avoiding violence and using a stealth dynamic instead.[33] His argument, however, overlooks why players are provided a weapon in the first place. A focus on stealth and pacifism doesn't negate violence as key to the FPS genre. For even if a player chooses (or tries) to avoid committing carnage themselves, the enemies will retaliate nonetheless.

Narrative

In Brian Upton's *Aesthetics of Play*, in order to use game studies to critique and inform literary studies, he starts his analysis "anchored firmly in much older critical and philosophical traditions".[34] Like Upton, rather than "trying to protect game studies from being colonized by literary studies" for this analysis I want to adapt traditional narrative theories with medium-specificity in mind. Some of those differences include video games non-linear, procedural, interactive, and ergodic nature.[35] This isn't a radical concept. Narrative scholar H. P. Abbott brought attention to the difference between literary narratives and video games in an aside for his primer, *The Cambridge Introduction to Narrative*. For Abbott, the bare minimum definition of narrative is "the representation of an event or a series of events".[36] These events or sequence of events constitute the text's story and the narrative discourse is "how the story is conveyed.[37] By this definition, story and narrative discourse share a similar emerging relationship to mechanics and dynamics by Hunicke's formulation. A game's narrative discourse is determined by how the rules at play (mechanics) are played (dynamics). But a video game's dynamics are not static. Per our earlier *Dishonored* example, a player may experience a different narrative discourse based on their dynamic choices. If the player executes a guard, then his comrades might hear the struggle and be alerted to Corvo's presence. If the player chooses patience's, they may overhear more of a guards' conversation and learn precious info that could effect their choice of actions ahead, altering the direction of the game.

How can this multiplicity be resolved? This issue brings attention to the necessity to bear medium-specificity in mind. For Abbott, Espen Aarseth's *Cybertext* answers the "role-playing conundrum" in a manner that is compatible and evolves somewhat seamlessly from traditional definitions of narrative. For Aarseth, a sequence of events is not a story, but actions. These actions or ergodic, "situation in which a chain of events… has been produced by nontrivial efforts of one or more mechanisms.[38] These ergodic chains of events created by the player's actions or interactivity produce "intrigue," events singular to each player based on their dynamic choices:

> [Rather] than a fixed story with its linear course, there are multiple possibilities, and that particular series of events that actually happens is recorded in the manner of a log: Instead of a narrative constituted of a story or plot, we get an intrigue-oriented ergodic log.[39]

For this analysis, when discussing the events of the games installed by the developers prior to the gamers playing, traditional literary terms (ex. story, plot, narrative) will be used. Aarseth's terminology will be used when discussing events of the game dependent upon players' interactions.

Ludonarrative Dissonance

The explicit connection between narrative and ludology as it pertains to *BioShock* is not a revolutionary premise. Clint Hocking, former level designer, game designer, and scriptwriter for Ubisoft Montreal, frequently blogged about his experiences as a developer on his personal website, *Click Nothing: Design From a Long Time Ago*. His argument in "Ludonarrative Dissonance in *BioShock*" is *BioShock* suffered "from a powerful dissonance between what it is about as a game, and what it is about as a story."[40] I concur with Hocking's premise; however, it is the narrative and ludological components that Hocking chooses to examine where I find his piece lacking. Hocking's post was hardly informed or productive. He only uses the phrase "ludonarrative dissonance" once, in the title, thus a firm definition of his term, or how he defines ludology and/or narratology is never provided. It can be surmised that ludonarrative dissonance refers to the gap between "what a text is about as a game and what it is about as a story."[41]

Hocking's blog post gave rise to a debate that previously had been of little consequence: how narrative and gameplay are at odds in video games. According to Espen Aarseth, editor-in-chief of *Game Studies*, this argument is:

> used as a touchstone by beginners to prove they know their way around the field, but—without exception, the writer doesn't have a clue, and the paper is typically about something entirely unrelated to the issue of whether games

> are narratives or not. What it does signal is that the writer feels the need to blend in, to show that they are aware of some stuff that has gone before (in those murky days of 1998–2001), but the effect is that they end up perpetuating the myth that there was a group of narrative theorists who had a quarrel with another group called 'ludologists'. (This is not the place to explain that great misunderstanding, instead see Aarseth 2014, but suffice it to say that the so-called ludologists were all using narratology, whereas the so-called narratologists were not, with the possible exception of a little bit of Aristotle.) This is not at all to suggest that there should be no more discussion of the relation between games and stories, because there is very little actual, informed, productive disagreement in our field, both on that topic and many others, and room for much more. Direct, vocal criticism is, or should be, a sign of respect. So perhaps there is too little of both?[42]

Despite the lack of scholarly context, after Hocking published his blog post, the term was reused and repurposed by academics of various disciplines and journalists alike. Computer scientist and physicists Mikael Hansson and Stefan Karlsson in their study, "A Matter of Perspective: A Qualitative study of Player-presence in First-person Video Games" used ludonarrative dissonance as "a perceived disconnect by the player, brought on by inconsistencies between actions required of the player, through a game's ludology, and a narrative story portrayed within the fiction context," but they do not define what constitutes ludology.[43] Military entertainment scholar Matthew Payne describes ludonarrative dissonance in *War Bytes: The Critique of Militainment in Spec Ops: The Line* as a "disaffected state".[44] Sociologist Scott Hughes' essay "Get real: Narrative and gameplay in 'The Last of Us'" uses the term ludonarrative dissonance in the abstract and is listed as a keyword, but like Hocking he never actually uses it in his article.

While Hocking's term has become common usage for players, developers, critics, journalists, and academics, not all agree with its application. Semionaut and narrative designer Corvus Elrod regarded the term as pointless and redundant. For example, "we have a situation where the fight choreography does not uphold the fiction behind the show. But don't refer to this as choreonarrative dissonance. Nor, for that matter, do we refer to the poorly written and delivered dialog as dialonarrative dissonance. Or the lackluster camera work as cinemanarrative dissonance.[45] *Grantland*'s resident video game journalist Tom Bissell agrees that "some designers and critics regard ludonarrative dissonance as a core problem in modern game design".[46] Despite these objections, the term continues to be used in game reviews, criticisms, and scholarly articles.

Ludonarrative Synchronicity

It is not my intention to continue in Hocking's footsteps, but to co-opt this popular usage of "ludonarrative". Rather than using Hocking's term, "ludonarrative dissonance," which is loaded with negative connotation, I will analyze the *BioShock* franchise based on their attempt to reach "ludonarrative synchronicity." Instead of assessing whether a video game "manages to successfully marry their ludic and narrative themes into a consistent and fully realized whole," ludonarrative synchronicity is designed to analyze how the ludic/gameplay and narrative themes interact, whether in harmony or at odds, to create a subject.[47] To determine ludonarrative synchronicity, I will be using a refined version of the inquiry into drama in games set forth by Marc LeBlanc, who worked with Ken Levine at Looking Glass Studios.[48] According to LeBlanc, the topic of this essay "comes from [his] first lecture at the Game Developer's Conference (GDC) in 1999… At that time, it was becoming clear that our discourse on game design needed more of a conceptual framework".[49] LeBlanc's analysis is founded on three questions: How does the narrative function create affect? What kinds of dynamics can evoke the narrative? From what kinds of mechanics do those dynamics emerge? These inquiries are "a way to place individual topics of discussion in their proper aesthetic context".[50] In the case of this analysis, the individual topics of discussion, or subjects created, are choice and control. To explore how choice and control are played out narratively and ludologically, there are three specific facets of the *BioShock* titles that I wish to direct my focus on: theme, level design, and immersion.

Theme

Theme is a literary term that refers to "the main idea, or the central generalization, implied or stated in a work… made tangible through its depiction in character, action and imagery."[51] *Spec Ops: The Line* (2012), a loose adaptation of the film *Apocalypse Now* (itself an even looser adaptation of Conrad's novella, *Heart of Darkness*), has an anti-war theme that is exhibited in multiple ways. *Spec Ops* features multiple military characters with shady pasts, forces them to take drastic action that could doom the lives of innocents to save others, and features a gritty landscape of destruction brought upon Dubai by U.S. forces. While theme tends to best be exhibited by the narratological components of a game, the ludological elements can also be representative of its theme as well. Another theme in *Spec Ops: The Line*, and its two sources of influence, is a descent into darkness. This is represented by the game's level design, as the player *literally* descends from a higher elevation of the city buried in sand, set on saving the citizenry, before reaching Dubai's lowest point and having gone mad.

Level Design

In its simplest form, level design is

> the data entry and layout portion of the game development cycle. A level is, for all intents and purposes, the same as a mission, stage, map or other venue of the player interaction. As a level designer, you are chiefly responsible for the gameplay.[52]

According to designer Bart Vossen, specifically regarding the gameplay aspect of level design:

> Level design refers to the space in which the combat takes place. This includes the shape of the area, placement of objects and other gameplay elements in the area. It also partially includes which enemies are encountered, because these alter the mode of interaction and experience of the space.[53]

Level design is also about flow. Sigeru Miyamoto, creator of *The Legend of Zelda*, *Mario*, and numerous other Nintendo franchises, puts focus on directing the player in his level design. There are four goals he aims for in designing levels for the benefit of the player. The first is level flow. How do the spaces in the level fit together? Where is the player supposed to go, and will she know how to get there? Next is intensity ramping. Does the intensity of the experience ramp up in a satisfying way? Do monsters get more difficult as the level goes on? Does the player get a chance to learn how the enemies work and then display her mastery later? Third is variety. Is there sufficient variety in the gameplay? Do enemy encounters frequently repeat themselves? Are the spaces varied in interesting ways? Finally, is training. If the design requires new skills from the player, does it teach and test those skills appropriately?[54]

Level design can also be applied to a game's architecture, its aesthetic style, and the ambiance it creates. Even the smallest of details, a throwaway prop, can have significance and purpose in the game's level design. In 2013's *The Last of Us* remnants from life as we know it, before the zombie apocalypse in game, remain for the player to find. While running away from dangerous Clickers and other undead abominations, protagonist Joel becomes trapped on a college campus. Sneaking from room to room, it almost feels as if the occupants have just vacated for spring break, not that they are dead or worse. Trash is strewn across sticky carpet floors, food left out, but occasionally, Joel will come across a panicked note written on the wall asking for help. These details add to the affect of fear, reminding the player just how quickly death can come in this game.

Immersion

Immersion is neither strictly narratological or ludological at its core and has two applications in video game studies. The player getting "caught up in the world of the game's story" is an example of immersion at the diegetic level, while the player's love of the game and the strategy that goes into it is immersion at the nondiegetic level."[55] For the former form of immersion, a fully developed diegesis is more important than one with realistic visuals or sounds. According to Janet Murray, "the more realized the immersive environment, the more active we want to be within it. When things we do bring tangible results, we experience... [a] sense of agency."[56] In *Goldeneye* (1997), even though the toilets resemble cubist art gone array and their flushing sound is hardly apropos, the veil of reality is maintained by the sensory feedback players get when pressing a button causes a toilet to flush. It is a simple mechanic but helps maintain the illusion of the game's reality, its diegesis.

The latter form of immersion, at the nondiegetic level, will be analyzed by means of player's relationship with their avatar. As mentioned in the "Tutorial" section "an avatar is a graphical figure like a character in a video game," but also according to Janet Murray avatars are a "mask that creates the boundary of the immersive reality and signals that we are role-playing rather than acting as ourselves".[57] In the *BioShock* trilogy, this boundary is blurred to different degrees as whether or not the player is fully in control of their avatar and whether or not the choices they make are influenced by the avatar's background. A majority of FPSs' stories start with avatars in media res, already experiencing the game's overall narrative. For the purpose of this ludonarrative synchronic analysis a fourth dramatic inquiry could be asked: "does the game start (with the pre-defined narrative) and end (through the player's intrigue-oriented ergodic log") with the same avatar-player relationship.

Research Approach & Analysis

> As game designers, we need a way to analyze games, to try to understand them, and to understand what works and what makes them interesting. We need a critical language. And since this is basically a new form, despite its tremendous growth and staggering diversity, we need to invent one.[58]

In the sixteen years since Greg Costikyan laid down the theoretical gauntlet, numerous designers and scholars have attempted to develop the Holy Grail of methodologies. Similar to defining terms, this is no simple task nor is there a "correct" answer. With ludonarrative synchronicity as our methodology, I will be performing close readings of the three *BioShock* texts as our main method. The seminal reader *Understanding Video Games* recommends Susana Tosca's "Reading Resident Evil-Code Veronica X" as an example of a "close reading [that] employed textual analysis, closely examining the work, looking for noteworthy properties of the game's structure, and teasing out the meaning of the game's story".[59,60] While this type of analysis is commonplace amongst literary and film scholars, *Understanding Video Games* emphasizes how rare individualized examination of game titles are. Tosca's paper proposes a close "reading" of the computer game in a practical attempt to argue for the application of reader response criticism to digital media.

Beyond the close reading, I will use opinions from outside sources as well to judge the ludonarrative synchronicity of each game, including those in the press, other developers, and gamers. From pre-production to release, Irrational Games was open to revealing the process behind the making of their games, including releasing primary resources such as their original pitch for *BioShock*. Levine and other heads of departments remain open to the press and continue to discuss their past projects with journalists. I will be using these interviews and articles written by the developers themselves as primary resources to support my analysis. The purpose of bringing in the perspective of other critics, developers, and gamers is to assist in eliminating the possibility of a single subjective decision on whether the video game aligns with itself. In the video game industry, unlike film and literary critics, the opinions of reviewers, journalists, and even players can have a direct impact on the project they are covering. A video game is malleable and can be modified even after its initial release. When *Assassin's Creed Unity* was released November 11, 2014, early reviews of the game were critical of the many bugs and programming errors that rendered the game unplayable. Initial sales did not meet projections and only two weeks after the game's launch, Ubisoft Montreal CEO Yannis Mallet released an apology.

> Unfortunately, at launch, the overall quality of the game was diminished by bugs and unexpected technical issues. I want to sincerely apologize on behalf of Ubisoft and the entire *Assassin's Creed* team. These problems took away from your enjoyment of the game, and kept many of you from experiencing the game at its fullest potential. We've been working hard to fix the problems players are reporting, and the patches we have released so far have resolved many of them.[61]

Not all studios are as quick to respond to the wishes of fans or even respond at all. This is where "mods" come into play. "Mods" refers to modifications to games made by players, not the original developers. For instance, players have changed third-person camera games like *Grand Theft Auto V* (2013) into first-person games. The ability of the players to adjust games to fit their own wants and desires puts added pressures on studios to produce what the marketplace demands. For if the major companies are not producing the types of games desired by the audience, then critics and players well-versed in coding will.

Due to the unique nature shared by developers, gamers, and critics within the gaming industry, relevant criticism and observations made by those not associated with the *BioShock* teams are applicable for this analysis. Katie Salen and Eric Zimmerman's *The Game Design Reader: A Rules of Play Anthology* includes not only references to the work of scholars such as Henry Jenkins and developers like Mark LeBlanc, but also anonymous players known only by their handles such as Mochan's "The Evil Summoner FAQ_v1.0: How to Be a Cheap Ass." The piece falls under the category of "New Games Journalism" (NGJ), a term created by *Rock, Paper, Shotgun's* founder Kieron Gillen as an extension of Tom Wolfe's "The New Journalism."[62] The purpose of NGJ is to justify more personal-style writings on video games, rather than just the traditional form of criticism and reviews. "Bow, Nigger" by Ian Shanahan, also known as always black, is an example of NGJ that also appears in *The Game Design Reader*. These outside sources serve as touchstones for evaluating my own personal observations that may appear to cross the line between opinion and NGJ.

The following three chapters is devoted to a single game in the series, based on their release order: *BioShock*, *BioShock 2* and *BioShock Infinite*.[63] After connecting the particular text to its gaming historical context, each chapter will preview the game's core ludological components (mechanics-dynamics-affect) and narratological elements (narrative, story, characters, etc.). Once the premise of each title is established, the chapters will cover how choice & control are exhibited by means of the game's level design, theme, and level of immersion. These aspects will then be evaluated through a ludonarrative synchronicity analysis as to whether they form the subject of player's choice and control.

The strength of analyzing the *BioShock* trilogy in depth, rather than focusing on a group of separate, unrelated titles, is two-fold. First, having three, related games to analyze is that it allows for multiple interrelated points of comparison and correlation that appear in all three games. The other advantage is Ken Levine's stated goal for the franchise was to achieve some form of ludonarrative synchronicity, at least in the spirit of the as yet un-coined term.

Notes

1. All financial data acquired from IGN's 2007 Year in Review coverage.
2. Gabe Graziani, "BioShock (X360)," *GameSpy: BioShock Review*, August 16, 2007, https://web.archive.org/web/20071107015831/http://xbox360.gamespy.com/xbox-360/bioshock/813243p3.html.
3. Dan Griliopoulos, "BioShock," *XBOX 360: The Official Xbox Magazine*, August 24, 2007, https://web.archive.org/web/20071007024828/http://www.oxm.co.uk/article.php?id=1182.
4. Seth Schiesel, "Genetics Gone Haywire and Predatory Children in an Undersea Metropolis," *The New York Times*, September 8, 2007, http://www.nytimes.com/2007/09/08/arts/television/08shoc.html.
5. Peter Metzger, "*BioShock*? You're soaking in it," *Los Angeles Times*, September 20, 2007, http://articles.latimes.com/2007/sep/20/news/wk-gamea20.
6. Ken Levine, "From Shodan, to Big Daddy, to Elizabeth: The Evolution of AI Companions" (presentation, BAFTA, London, UK, March 11, 2013).
7. Brian Upton, *The Aesthetic of Play* (MIT Press, 2015), 12.

8. Espen Aarseth, "Computer Game Studies, Year One." *Game Studies*, 1, no. 1 (July 2007).
9. Gonzalo Frasca, "Ludology Meets Narratology: Similtude and differences between (video)games and narrative," *Ludology*, 1999, http://www.ludology.org/articles/ludology.html.
10. Ibid.
11. Robert Hunicke, et al. "MDA: A formal approach to game design and game research," (workshop, Game Developers Conference, San Jose, CA. 2001–2004).
12. Upton, 15.
13. Upton, 16.
14. This is, after all, the same game that describes a quasar grenade as E=mc^(OMG)/wtf.
15. Marc LeBlanc, "Tools for Creating Dramatic Game Dynamics," *The Game Design Reader: A Rules of Play Anthology* (Boston: MIT Press, 2006): 440.
16. LeBlanc, 441.
17. Mary Flanagan and Helen Nissenbaum, *Values at Play in Digital Games* (Boston: MIT Press, 2014), 70.
18. George Santayana, "What is Aesthetics?," *The Philosophical Review* 13, no. 3 (May 1904): 321.
19. Melissa Gregg and Gregory J. Seigworth. "An Inventory of Shimmers," *The Affect Theory Reader* (Durham: Duke UP, 2010), 2.
20. LeBlanc, 441.
21. Lawrence Grossberg, *Cultural Studies in the Future Tense* (Durham: Duke UP, 2010), 318.
22. Erik Kersting, "Competitive Depth and Exploitation in 'Sumer Smash Bros. Melee'," *Pop Matters*, last modified March 4, 2014, https://www.popmatters.com/competitive-depth-and-exploitation-in-super-smash-bros-melee-2495682315.html.
23. Ibid.
24. Mark J.P. Wolf, "Genre and the Video Game," in *The Medium of the Video Game!* ed. Mark J.P. Wolf (Austin: University of Texas Press, 2001), 113.
25. Ibid.
26. Janet Murray, *Hamlet on the Holodeck: The Future of Narrative in Cyberspace* (Cambridge: MIT Press, 1997), 113.
27. Alexander Galloway, *Gaming: Essays on Algorithmic Culture* (Minneapolis: University of Minnesota, 2006), xii.
28. Galloway, 41.
29. Fredric Jameson, *Signatures of the Visible* (New York: Routledge, 1992), 12.
30. Galloway, 43.
31. Galloway, 69.
32. Galloway, 57.

33. Galloway, 69.
34. Upton, 5.
35. Ibid.
36. Porter Abbott, *The Cambridge Introduction to Narrative* (Cambridge University Press, 2008), 13.
37. Abbott 15.
38. Espen Aarseth, *Cybertext: Perspectives on Ergodic Literature* (JHU Press, 1997), 113.
39. Ibid.
40. Hocking, "Ludonarrative Dissonance in *BioShock*."
41. Ibid.
42. Espen Aarseth, "Game Studies: How to Play – Ten Play-Tips for Aspiring Game-Studies Scholar," *Game Studies* 1, no. 1 (July 2007).
43. Mikael Hansson and Stefan Karlsson, "A Matter of Perspective: A Qualitative Study of Player-presence in First-person Video Games," Thesis, Umea University, 2016.
44. Matthew Payne, "War Bytes: The Critique of Militainment in *Spec Ops: The Line*," *Critical Studies in Media Communication* 31, no. 4 (2014): 269.
45. Eric Swain, "In Defense of Ludonarrative Dissonance," *The Game Critique* (blog), August 5, 2010. http://www.thegamecritique.com/recent-posts/in-defense-of-ludonarrative-dissonance/2283/.
46. Tom Bissell, "Vicodin Visions." *Grantland*, May 31, 2012, http://grantland.com/features/on-rockstar-games-max-payne-3/.
47. Hocking.
48. LeBlanc, 441.
49. LeBlanc, 438.
50. Ibid.
51. John M. Desmond and Peter Hawkes, *Adaptation: Studying Film & Literature* (New York: McGraw-Hill, 2006), 24.
52. Tim Ryan, "Beginning Level Design, Part 1," *Gamasutra*, April 16, 1999, http://www.gamasutra.com/view/feature/131736/beginning_level_design_part_1.php.
53. Bart Vossen, "Level design for melee combat systems," *Gamasutra*, March 24, 2015, http://gamasutra.com/blogs/BartVossen/20150324/239562/Level_design_for_melee_combat_systems.php.
54. Mike Stout, "Learning From The Masters: Level Design In *The Legend of Zelda*," *Gamasutra*, January 3, 2012, http://www.gamasutra.com/view/feature/134949/learning_from_the_masters_level_.php.
55. Alison McMahan, "Immersion, Engagement, and Presence: A Method for Analyzing 3-D Video Games," in *The Video Game Theory Reader*, ed. Mark

J.P. Wolf and Bernard Perron (New York: Routledge, Taylor & Francis Group, 2003), 68.
56. Murray, 126.
57. Murray, 113.
58. Greg Costikyan, "I Have No Words & I Must Design," *The Game Design Reader: A Rules of Play Anthology* (Cambridge: The MIT Press, 2006), 196.
59. Simon Egenfeldt-Nielsen, Jonas Heide Smith, and Susana Pajares Tosca, *Understanding Video Games: The Essential Introduction* (New York: Routledge, 2016), 10.
60. Tosca, Susan. "Reading Resident Evil-Code Veronica X." In *Proceedings of DAC03*. Melbourne: RMIT Press, 2003.
61. Yannis Mallet, "An Update on Assassin's Creed Unity from Yannis Mallat," *Assassin's Creed Live Updates*, November 26, 2014, http://assassinscreed.ubi.com/en-us/news/news_detail.aspx?c=tcm:154-186654-16&ct=tcm:148-76770-32.
62. Kieron Gillen, "The New Games Journalism," *Kieron Gillen's Workblog*, May 13, 2005, http://gillen.cream.org/wordpress_html/assorted-essays/the-new-games-journalism/.
63. This analysis will not explore the multiplayer portion of *BioShock 2*, nor do a separate in-depth analysis of any of the games' downloadable content (DLCs).

CHAPTER 2

BioShock: Welcome to Rapture

Abstract This chapter covers the original *BioShock*'s historical context and core ludological/narratological elements. It focuses on how choice and control are formed through the gameplay and story, asking whether or not players's truly get a say in the game's direction.

Keywords Choice • Control • Level design • Immersion • Theme • Ayn Rand • Objectivism

From 1996 to 2001 the marketplace for first-person shooters struggled. In '96 only twenty-two FPS titles were released. This lull continued into the twenty-first century, with an average of twenty-two FPSs released a year. Just as the genre appeared a lost cause, it shot back up in popularity, raising from twenty-three titles in 2001 to thirty-eight in 2002. The high-point of this era was in 2005, when fifty-five FPSs were made available. In 2006, *Gamasutra* reported the first-person shooter as one of the biggest and fastest growing video game genres in terms of revenue for publishers.[1] Much of this increase was due to the arrival of the seventh-generation consoles such as the XBOX 360 in 2005 and the PlayStation 3 in 2006. There was a small dip or valley between '06 to '08, but the average number of titles released still averaged forty-three games a year, including *BioShock* in 2007.

L. Reblin-Renshaw, *Ludonarrative Synchronicity in the 'BioShock' Trilogy*, https://doi.org/10.1007/978-3-030-63868-9_2

What set *BioShock* apart from the other shoot 'em up of its day, such as *Prey* (2006), *Crysis* (2007), and numerous *Call of Duty* titles, was the game's intricate narrative. *BioShock* did not just have a complex intricate story, but also the narrative altered based on the player's experience. The choices players made changed the game, and not just in an immediate sense, such as an enemy's head blown off and a fountain of blood spurts after a player press X to fire the grenade launcher. *BioShock*'s ending depended entirely on how the player chose to play the game. Would they be ruthless and brutal? Would they try to maintain some moral center? *BioShock* was not the first game to feature multiple conclusions. As far back as the early 1980s, games altered the end based on the character created by the player, particularly in computer role-playing games (CRPGs). The space-marine RPG *Mass Effect*, also released in 2007, carried the player's choices through not only the game, but also the entirety of the series. A choice made at the beginning of the first *Mass Effect* could effect events that occurred in *Mass Effect 3* (2012). A well-crafted CRPG, according Matt Barton, requires

> a diverse set of skills, such as tactics, long-term planning, problem solving… and resource management. Some CRPGs demand advanced navigation and even cartography skills; otherwise, players will end up hopelessly lost in a maze or dungeon. Others are loaded with puzzles and riddles. A few punish players not only for losing but also for winning in an unethical way.[2]

BioShock featured all of these elements, but as a FPS retaining a primary focus and mechanic on the violent shooting-based combat. A common criticism towards first-person shooters is that violence in these games lacked consequence. Their level of conflict was shallow. This could be achieved by having the opposition "unclearly defined, just there to represent darkness against the heroes".[3] Enemies could also be portrayed as "caricatures in [their] unwillingness to see reason".[4] With grey morality and complex characters, Ken Levine found a way to have both the story and the shooting by "re-inventing the first-person action RPG" with *BioShock*.[5]

A Modern Day Atlantis

BioShock's narrative begins in 1946, in the depths of the Atlantic, where a business magnate's dream was finally founded. Andrew Ryan constructed his Objectivism-based utopia as an escape from the parasites of the surface world: the communists of Russia, the socialists in America, and the religious fervor that Ryan felt halted the sciences and arts.

> What is the difference between a man and a parasite? A man builds. A parasite asks, "Where is my share?" A man creates. A parasite says, "What will the neighbors think?" A man invents. A parasite says, "Watch out, or you might tread on the toes of God."[6]

Therefore, Ryan built the impossible: Rapture. For over a decade, though cut-off from the rest of modern society, the underwater city thrived. Then, Rapture became a nightmare. Its laissez-faire policies created an irreversible economic gap and soon the lower class had had enough. It became clear though, after one failed revolt, that the less fortunate needed their own non-economic source of power. Frank Fontaine, thought killed in the failed coup, controlled the supply of ADAM in the city. This chemical compound was the base ingredient for plasmids, which gave users superhuman abilities. Now, hiding amongst the poor under the alias Atlas, Fontaine created an army of ADAM-junkies, driven insane from the overuse of plasmids. A Rapturian's financial status no longer mattered. If you bled, you'd be dead.

The game's story and the player ergodic journey begins in 1960, where Jack, the sole survivor of a plane crash, is lost at sea in the Atlantic Ocean. Whether by fate or pure luck, Jack finds his way to the hidden underwater city of Rapture. The former Objectivism utopia has fallen into disarray forcing Jack into the fray as he battles his way through demented Splicers, citizens addicted to ADAM, and traps laid by Rapture's architect, Andrew Ryan. Jack is befriended by the revolutionist Atlas, who aids Jack with instructions, hoping that in guiding Jack through Rapture he can use him to save his own family from Ryan's wrath.[7] Or that's the story the story as Jack (and the player) knows it.

Ken Levine, along with co-directing the game with Alyssa Finley, was also *BioShock*'s writer. Levine put his "useless liberal arts degree" to work and created a narrative influenced by a wide-range of "utopian and distopian [sic]" writers such as Aldous Huxley, George Orwell, and especially

Ayn Rand.[8] Rapture's founders based their tenants on the Randian philosophy of Objectivism and its core principles: individualism, freedom, rationality, and capitalism.[9] The plot of *BioShock* shares multiple parallels to that of Ayn Rand's 1957 novel, *Atlas Shrugged*. Andrew Ryan, whose name is a partial anagram for Ayn Rand, shares her disillusionment with America after her escape from Russia, and he is also Rapture's John Galt from *Atlas Shrugged*. In the novel, Galt's Gulch is a "capitalist utopia… where the great titans of the era have been hiding. Here reside the preeminent industrialists, financiers, builders, jurists, scientists, composers, and artists who have vanished over a twelve-year period."[10] Dagny Taggart, the novel's protagonist, does not discover the hideaway until she is involved in a plane crash that just happens to occur near the location, similar to the opening of *BioShock* and Jack's happenstance upon Rapture. Dr. Robert Stadler, one of *Atlas Shrugged*'s antagonists, has a Rapturian counterpart in Frank Fontaine. Like Stadler's betrayal of Galt, Fontaine worked for Ryan initially to gain Rapture's secrets and sell them to the United States government. It is with Stadler, a prototypical mad scientist that the novel "borders on science fiction."[11] Fontaine too has a knack for kooky science, discovering the mysterious substance ADAM for which he later teams up with Dr. Brigid Tenenbaum to create Little Sisters as vessels to generate and harvest the rare material.

Little Sisters are young girls that appear as greyish corpses with glowing yellow eyes, another monstrous result of a society "where the scientist would not be bound by petty morality."[12] They do not retain their minds in the conventional sense-they act like little girls in some regards, but who they were before is completely gone. Big Daddies are steampunk cyborgs, unlucky humans turned into horrific guardians of the Little Sisters. Along with being stuck in a massive diving suit, they are equipped with a large drill. Big Daddies are mini-bosses, enemies that are more difficult to fight than the common Splicer, and they appear repeatedly throughout the game, but only one or two times per level. The Big Daddies and Little Sisters, with their monstrous forms, exemplify the affect Irrational Games was aiming for. *BioShock* will "tell a mature, terrifying story," the initial game pitch says, and it will "scare the hell out of people."[13] There are other ways, beyond character design, that *BioShock* affirms its nightmarish experience or affect. The level design, as shall be discussed, creates an environment in which there is imminent danger lurking behind every corner and the player must be wary of an enemy attack, maintaining tension throughout the game. However, unlike other popular FPS survival horror games, such as *Amnesia: The Dark Descent* (2010) or *Five Nights at Freddy's* (2014) that leave the player weaponless, in *BioShock* the player is given the means to fight back through a trio of mechanics.

BioShock features three main mechanics: shooting, hacking, and harvesting/rescuing. The core mechanic of the game is shooting. A major dynamic portion of the game is the player's choice of what to shoot. Players can choose between the traditional style of shooting, various weapons, different ammo for those weapons, and even the combat alternative to use super-human power-ups called plasmids, instead of traditional guns. Another mechanic featured in *BioShock* is the ability to hack various machinery. The earliest vision for *BioShock* influences this portion of the gameplay.[14] According to the original pitch document:

> Carlos Cuello, a down and out "deprogrammer" is assigned to infiltrate a religious cult on a remote island and "rescue" a wealthy heiress from the clutches of the cultists. Once on the island, however, you find out that all is not as it seems.[15]

A previous title Irrational Game created, *System Shock 2*, which in turn was a sequel to a title Levine worked on at his old company, Looking Glass Studios, was the basis for the hacking system. While the initial design documents do not divulge the mechanical process for hacking into the security terminals, it does provide the results of such actions.

> Once into the system the player can do a variety of things [such as] shut down or take control of security turrets, set off false alarms to divert the enemy's attention, or commandeer security robots and control them and their powerful arsenal remotely. Players lose control of their avatar but get a first-person perspective from the robot and now control it directly. But be careful, your avatar is helpless while in control of the robot.[16]

Because the use of indirect control is antithetical to the game's stated intention of control, a break in ludonarrative synchronicity, the remote-control robots were eventually scrapped. As stated in the initial game pitch, "*BioShock* gives the player absolute control; of their environments as well as in the creation of their own weapons and bio-modifications. The only limit is their imagination."[17]

The game intends to emphasize player's sense of dominance and control over the avatar and game. The mechanic that provides the player with the strongest sense of control over the game, including its narrative and player's intrigue-oriented ergodic log, is the choice to rescue or harvest the Little Sisters after defeating their hulking, metal guardians. For programmer and video game blogger Brendan Vance:

> The city of Rapture feels to me like a place built by deduction. Centering on the crucial dynamic between Big Daddies and Little Sisters the studio extrapolated outward; every aspect of the city, from characters like Andrew Ryan to the citizens' Objectivist worldview, serves to focus and complicate the dynamic.[18]

The relationship between these two characters has as much to do with narratology as it does ludology and thus leads us to our first key point of ludonarrative synchronicity thematically.

In the End, Our Choices Make Us

In a series of interviews for *Critical Path*, Robin Hunicke states:

> Games are about choice. They are about giving you meaningful choices. Because games are about meaningful choices, they can be about empowering choices, but they don't necessarily have to be about that.[19]

Choice is featured everywhere in the *BioShock* universe. Gamers are always making dynamic choices during gameplay. Jump here or walk there? Shoot that or knife this? However, the use of choice in the *BioShock* series takes the concept beyond those featured in a typical FPS. Not only can the player choose how to fight, but also what skills to choose, more in keeping in line with an RPG game. Choices made have immediate results via the gameplay, but over time by means of the narrative as well. The ending is a product of these choices. It is not just how the player chooses to play dynamically, but whom the player chooses to be morally.

In *BioShock*, the moral dilemma is whether to harvest the creepy Little Sisters or to rescue them. After defeating a Big Daddy, an event where a great deal of ammo, health, and ADAM is expended, the player is forced to make this difficult decision. Precious resources, however, are not drained during the first encounter with a Little Sister who has lost her Big Daddy. The player observes a Splicer attacking a Little Sister, only to witness the ADAM-junkie shot by Dr. Tenenbaum. The Little Sister's creator pleads: "*Bitte*, do not hurt her! Have you no heart?"[20] Atlas, who up to this point in the game has been a reliable guide, also appeals to the player's empathy. "You won't survive without the ADAM those... things... are carrying. Are you prepared to trade your life, the lives of my wife and child for Tenenbaum's little Frankenstein's?"[21] As the Little Sister crawls into a corner, terrified, the following instructions appear on screen:

> CHOOSE whether to RESCUE the Little Sister or HARVEST her. If you harvest her, you get MAXIMUM ADAM to spend on plasmids, but she will NOT SURVIVE the process. If you rescue her, you get LESS ADAM, but Tenenbaum has promised to make it WORTH YOUR WHILE.

The Objectivist choice would be to gain the full wealth of resources and harvest the Little Sister. The "right" decision to do is unclear. The player must choose between helping the doctor and her subjects, who up until this point have been portrayed as merely a mad scientist and her monstrous creations or help oneself in order to save the seemingly trustworthy Atlas and his family. That is the narratological side of the quandary.

The ludological side is a matter of resource management. Due to on-screen advisement, the player is aware of what the prize will be for harvesting, while the rescuing option is unclear in regard to not only how much less ADAM one receives but also what "worth your while" actually means. As previously mentioned, besides the first encounter with a Little Sister, the rescuing/harvesting option presents a crucial dynamic choice that appears to affect the difficulty of the gameplay for the moments following. Or does it? A player, going by the handle Ajar, posted on *The Escapist* web forum a quibble he had while playing through *BioShock* the first time. After rescuing all of the Little Sisters during his initial run of the game, Ajar was left wondering "why [he] wasn't feeling constrained by a lack of ADAM."[22] In order to answer his own question, Ajar performed a theorycrafting analysis. According to sociologist Bonni Nardi, whose research found her engaged as a participant in the act of playing *Word of Warcraft*, theorycrafting is "the discovery of rules that cannot be determined through play."[23] I would argue that theorycrafting is the process of breaking down a game's mechanics via an analytically focused dynamic playstyle. The *Elitist Jerk* website, dedicated to thoughtful technical discussions pertaining to *World of Warcraft*, provides examples:

> Posts demonstrate that players played a game about the game in which they attempted to figure out the game's own machinations. Technically oriented players designed quantitative experiments, performed tests, analyzed the results, published them online, and worked with one another to solve puzzles of game mechanics.[24]

After multiple replays, Ajar concluded that harvesting rewards the player with 160 ADAM per Little Sister, while rescuing gives the player 80 ADAM per Little Sister plus 200 ADAM from Tenenbaum every third Little Sister saved and other rewards that were not specified when presented with the choice.

> The difference trends toward 10% of what you get by rescuing. For instance, after 16 Little Sisters rescued the player has accrued 2280 ADAM. After 16 Little Sisters harvested, the player has accrued 2560 ADAM, a difference of 280 (12%). Also, you get the Hypnotize Big Daddy plasmids, which are extremely valuable and can't be acquired any other way, along with other ancillary benefits (various gene tonics, ammunition, health kits).[25]

Ajar's theory as to "why this is still presented as an ethical dilemma," despite mathematically not being so, is that "you don't know the rewards at the outset."[26] The player does not know that technically "harvesting is a less effective game strategy overall."[27] Nor does the player know how rescuing versus harvesting affects the story (sans spoilers). How the Little Sisters are treated is the basis for the conclusion presented. *BioShock* has three possible endings. If the player chooses to rescue all the Little Sisters, then Jack and several Little Sisters escape Rapture to live normal lives.

If the player chooses to harvest all the Little Sisters, then Jack and several Splicers escape Rapture to destroy the surface world with the terrible secrets he has stolen.

Even if the player harvests only one Little Sister, Jack becomes a villain, but Tenenbaum's condemnation of his actions is less virulent than if he destroyed all her girls. The presence of these three endings creates a unique experience for the player in two ways. First, there is an incentive to replay the game. Perhaps first time around the player chooses to play the game empathetically and now they want to see if Jack can progress more easily through Rapture with more ADAM in hand. The other benefit to the multiple endings is that they make the player feel as if their choices mattered. Thus ludonarrative synchronicity, in regard to the importance of choice, is maintained.

Somewhere Beyond the Sea

Just as the works of Ayn Rand influence the plot of *BioShock*, so do her books inspire the level design. Andrew Ryan built Rapture in 1946, but the city's design is that of the popular Art Deco movement that rose to prominence in the 1920s and 1930s. The use of the term Art Deco did not come "into general usage [until] soon after a 1966 exhibition, 'Les Années "25" Art Deco/Bauhas/Stijl/Esprit Nouveau,' presented at the Musée des Arts Decoratifs, Paris."[28] Instead, the movement was often referred to as the modern style.[29] If Art Deco was the term of the times when Rand published *The Fountainhead* in 1943, surely its protagonist Howard Roark and his buildings would have been categorized as part of the movement. In the novel, Roark is an architect who fights against the neoclassical style. Roark does not have a direct counterpart in *BioShock*, but he does in real life. Rand studied "the masters of early skyscraper design and of clean, fluid modernist styling, Louis Sullivan and Frank Lloyd Wright."[30] While Sullivan, the grand architect of the Chicago skyscraper, was the basis for the character of Henry Cameron in *The Fountainhead*, Wright's "organic architectural style, his emphasis on "Truth in Architecture," his contempt for imitation and mediocrity, [and] his transcendent indifference to clients' good opinion" became the foundation for Roark. Wright's work, or even those of his fictional counterpart, would have fit in seamlessly to the Rapture landscape, which highlights Art Deco's trademarks such as:

> geometric elements, handsome ornamental metalwork, classical yet unmistakably modern, sculptures and reliefs, generous use of colour (in terracotta ornament, metal, paint, stone and even stained glass) and their imaginative juxtaposition of light-and-dark and matte-and-textured elements.[31]

While aesthetically pleasing, this level design also affects the difficulty of gameplay, thus having both a narratological and ludological impact. In Rapture, Splicer's footsteps can be heard from a distance echoing off the tiled floors. The singing of hymns by Waders (blue-collar zealots) echo eerily through the empty halls, becoming terrible tunes warranting trepidation. The shadows of enemies' project upon the walls, made even ghastlier by the neon lights and ocean glow. Irrational Games meant *BioShock* to be a "horrifying, sophisticated, visually stunning… experience that would leave players gasping for breath" and the city of Rapture provides this affect with its architecture alone.[32]

Even the underwater setting hearkens back to *BioShock*'s literary influence. Dazzled by the cinema of America, at an early age Ayn Rand envisioned her future home as '"Atlantis:" the ideal existence for intelligent, purposeful, ruggedly individualist men and, presumably, women."[33] Sadly, that was not the case with the United States, so Rand created her Atlantis with Galt's Gulch. While his city was not underwater, the final act of *Atlas Shrugged*, in which John Galt finally reveals his mission, is titled "Atlantis."[34] Promotional material for *BioShock*, including a mockumentary entitled "Fact From Myth," referred to Rapture as a Modern Day Atlantis.[35] The decision to set the story underwater goes beyond narrative influence to provide a specific affect. Water, a representation of life for humans who require it to survive, is also representative of death in *BioShock*. The ocean is an ever-present danger to the citizens of Rapture. Any time a player passes by a cracked window, the threat abounds, and the water's pressure can be felt, both in a literal and figurative fashion. Water, the bringer of life and death, can be used to the benefit or the detriment of the player. At times, leaks in the structure block pathways. At other occasions, a flooded floor allows the player to use the plasmid Electro Bolt to electrocute enemies that are standing in the water (though be wary of shocking oneself if not on dry land). Other plasmids are water based such as Winter Blast; however, that freezing power does not require the actual presence of water nearby. The mechanic of hacking also has a water element to it. To hack a machine, security robot, or alarm, the player is required to complete a mini-game ala *Pipe Mania* (1989). The player must rearrange segments of tubes into the correct pattern so that when the timer goes off, water may flow to the exit drain without resistance.

The haunting aquatic beauty of Rapture more often works against the player than for them. The tight spaces, rather than an open layout, create a sense of claustrophobia, but also affect the combat dynamic. While the player has the option of using weapons such as a pistol, machine gun, shotgun, and even a grenade launcher, the small rooms are conducive to limited range combat. Distance-based weapons can be utilized, but the player also must be prepared for melee combat by use of a wrench whenever necessary as well. The numerous stairwells and columned hallways also create a lack of direct line of fire. The player must depend on the sense of hearing rather than vision- quickly peeking into the next room to sneak up upon enemies is both dangerous and difficult. Players are also limited regarding their movement. It is difficult to run away from an encounter once blood spills and there are few places to hide, especially in the atriums. These difficulties, however, do not represent poor level design, but design choices used to elevate the game's affect. It is a perilous balance, for fear can lead to frustration and frustration can lead to disgruntled players or provide satisfaction upon overcoming such grand challenges. There are ways to balance out the degree of difficulty. At times, Jack can traverse through levels without being attacked, giving the player time to enjoy the work put into the level design. Long interactions without the player feeling the need to act also allow the player a break from the violence, and while a sense of relief may wash over the players as they come upon a large room with open space, this change in level design signals an increased level of difficulty, commonly corresponding to a boss fight. These expansive areas put the player's skills to the test. For Vossen "boss fights and the arenas they take place in are usually tailor-made for each other."[36] It is not just that these encounters are combat specific, but level design-specific as well. Alex Schulman, combat designer for the *God of War* series, believes, "that boss design uses the environment really well and integrates the boss into the area or into the stage."[37]

This is played out both literally and figuratively during Jack's confrontation with Sander Cohen. Cohen is an artist and the minions featured in his level represent the arts. Fort Frolic, a district ruled by the crazed artist, used to be "where the best and brightest celebrate success," but has now become where the worst and hardest Splicers aggress. Besides the common Thuggish and Nitro Splicers, Fort Frolic is also home to Spider Splicers, whose acrobatic movements resemble those of a nimble dancer. There are also Houdini Splicers who can teleport. Sections of Fort Frolic have literal stages, such as the first part of the level that takes place in a theater, Fleet Hall. The player is aware that this is the first area they must visit, despite several other entrances in the two-level atrium, because the neon sign for Fleet Hall lights first and is the brightest. Over the radio Sander Cohen says that "the artist has a duty to seduce the ear" and as the player comes closer and closer to the map objective the music becomes clearer and louder. As the player advances through map objective to map objective before meeting Cohen face to face, Sander watches from above, whether it be from a theater booth or a darkened balcony. This gameplay is a performance for him. When Sander decides to reveal himself, he makes a grand entrance, either descending the staircase in the atrium or walking down from the second floor of his apartment "this interaction with the environment is often intuitively seen by players as signifier of a boss fight, and results in strong synergy between the enemy's behaviors and the level."[38] If the player chooses to fight Cohen (though this is not required to complete the level) then Sander has the abilities of a Houdini Splicer. Cohen's Houdini Splicer fighting style gives him the ability to teleport anywhere in not only an expansive region but a dual-levelled one as well, making him even more difficult than his Houdini Splicer minions.

A Man Chooses, A Slave Obeys

According to Janet Murray, "an avatar is a graphical figure like a character in a video game" but also "[a] mask that creates the boundary of the immersive reality and signals that we are role-playing rather than acting as ourselves."[39] Jack's avatar in *BioShock* is never fully seen, only his disembodied hands, thus preserving the immersive experience. Initially, however, the game has the player set in the position of observer rather than active participant, antithetical to Levine's stated goals. The prologue opens with narration by Jack, whose name is gathered by the camera panning down to a letter Jack is holding, along with a blurry photo of Jack featuring few discernable features. We hear Jack's voiceover as his flight hits stormy weather: "When Mum and Dad put me on that plane, they told me, 'Son, you're special, you were born to do great things.' You know what? They were right."[40] The plane then spins out of control, crashes and the player finally gains control of the avatar as Jack flounders in the water. This opening sequence, in the span of less than a minute, covers multiple manners of perspective. The scene takes place through Jack's eyes, a first-person point of view. The letter and photo set up Jack as a distinct entity, rather than an empty vessel for the player to fill.

The end of the game's second act covers the fluidity of identification more extensively. On his way to murder Andrew Ryan, Jack finds a board in the antagonist's office covered with photographs, papers, and the phrase "would you kindly" written out in red ink. This room is a visual illustration of Jack's backstory, but the player does not know that yet. Neither the player nor Jack understand why the mad scientists Yu Suchong and Tenenbaum, along with Andrew Ryan, and a beautiful woman all have threads connecting their photos to Jack's. Nor why an upside down black-filled headshot with a question mark on it is pinned to the photo of Jack as well. The writing on the wall, "would you kindly" is the equivalent of *The Shining's* "redrum." The message is obvious, after the fact.

The fact is that Jack is not who the player or he thinks he is. The player advances from the office to find Andrew Ryan, alone in Rapture Central Control. Ryan does not directly address Jack as the player walks in on him leisurely putting golf balls, the room collapsing around Ryan from prior explosives set.

> The assassin has overcome my final line of defense, and now he plans to murder me. In the end what separates a man from a slave? Money? Power? No, a man chooses, and a slave obeys!

The fourth wall is then broken as Ryan stops golfing and continues orating, keeping his eyes towards not just Jack, but at the screen as well.

> You think you have memories. A farm. A family. An airplane. A crash. And then this place. Was there really a family? Did that airplane crash, or, was it hijacked? Forced down, forced down by something less than a man, something bred to sleepwalk through life unless activated by a simple phrase, spoken by their kindly master.

The player is unable to control Jack, who begins to follow Ryan's every request.

> Would you kindly, powerful phrase. Familiar phrase? Sit, would you kindly? Stand, would you kindly? Run! Stop! Turn. Was a man sent to kill, or a slave? KILL! A man chooses! A slave obeys! OBEEEEEEY![41]

The game seems to have reached its climax. Andrew Ryan flays out on the ground, bludgeoned to death by Jack with his own golf club. The player and Jack now know the awful truth. They have been nothing but a tool for murder and mayhem. Just as Jack was incapable of dismissing Ryan's assisted suicide wish, the player is unable to resist the developer's manipulation. This brutal moment in *BioShock* is a critique of the FPS genre, of how players focus so much on achieving various goals, trophies, and objectives that they pay little attention to their emotional choices or lack thereof. Players have been brainwashed by the genre to become unquestioning agents of mass destruction, rather than possessing any agency of their own. However, just as suddenly as this revelation is bestowed upon the player, the narrative picks right back up, playing "itself out in objective-led fashion, expecting players to somehow forget what's just happened" for nearly another half of the game's runtime.[42]

According to Marc LeBlanc:

> The climax occurs at the moment of realization, when uncertainty is dispelled and the outcome of the contest is known. Given that definition, it would seem that the climax of the game should occur as late as possible. After all, a contest whose outcome is known has ceased to be a game on some level: the players have become spectators. We could argue that such an interval should be as short as possible.[43]

After the "Would You Kindly" reveal, the lapses in ludonarrative synchronicity become more apparent. When Tenenbaum saves Jack from the collapsing Rapture Control Center, she begins to deprogram Jack. However, while this does provide narrative reasoning for the player to regain agency, this deus ex machina moment does not necessarily make sense with a player's intrigue-oriented ergodic log. If the player has been rescuing the Little Sisters, Jack receiving Tenenbaum's assistance is a logical consequence for good behavior. However, Tenenbaum helps Jack regardless of how he has treated the Little Sisters. She assists Jack even if he has been harvesting the very girls she takes care of. The plot reveals itself, in what should be a moment of freedom for Jack and the player, to no longer be a player-driven narrative.

Summary

Overall, up until the "Would You Kindly" reveal, *BioShock* has multiple incidences of ludonarrative synchronicity. Narratively, the influence of Ayn Rand and her Objectivism philosophy is blended seamlessly into the characters, plot, and level design. The Art Deco sensibility gives rise to an affect of horror. The beauty of the environment hides just how dangerous a watery wonderland can be. As the story unfolds, the consequences of strict adherence to Ayn Rand's Objectivism reveal themselves. Left unchecked, a society based on individualism, freedom, rationality, and capitalism creates chaos. Not only does Jack/the player have to face off against enemies mutated by greed and unbounded by ethical norms, but is also placed in situations where Objectivist decisions are tempting. Harvest the Little Sisters for what seem to be valuable resources or maintain ones humanity by saving them? The effect ludologically through the Little System harvest/rescue mechanic is resource management, and affects the difficulty of the game and thus is a thematic and dynamic choice. The theme of choice appears in another mechanic/dynamic system, through combat and the use of multiple types of weapon and power-ups.

However, though the effective (and affective) level design elements remain present in the second half of the game, the theme of choice and level of immersion are rendered mute and breaks the internal logic of the game. Ken Levine himself admitted, "You had a situation there where you had this amazing character and once he's gone the story loses some of its steam."[44] If the game had proceeded directly towards Jack seeking out and killing Frank Fontaine, which is the eventual ending, then even though the game has brought into question the matter of agency, the player would still have been provided "with a dénouement to resolve the tension and give them a sense of closure."[45] Instead, *BioShock* both criticizes and falls victim to the faults of agency and morality in FPS, yet somehow still tries to present agency as an obtainable reality with the inclusion of multiple endings whose narrative are affected by players' choices in relationship to the Little Sisters.

Notes

1. Frank Cifaldi, "Analysts: FPS 'Most Attractive' Genre for Publishers," *Gamasutra*, 2006, https://www.gamasutra.com/view/news/99195/Analysts_FPS_Most_Attractive_Genre_for_Publishers.php.
2. Matt Barton, *Dungeons & Desktops: The History of Computer Role-Playing Games*, (A K Peters, Ltd. 2008), 2–3.
3. Martin Annander, "Boom, Headshot!," *Gamasutra* (2017), https://gamasutra.com/blogs/MartinAnnander/20170425/296704/Boom_Headshot.php.
4. Ibid.
5. IG. Admin, "From the Vault-The BioShock Pitch," *Irrational Games Insider*, May 20, 2010, http://irrationalgames.com/insider/from-the-vault-may/.
6. Andrew Ryan, "A Man or a Parasite," *Audio Diaries*, Hephaestus.
7. "BioShock," *BioShock Wiki*, http://*BioShock*.wikia.com/wiki/*BioShock*.
8. Douglass C. Perry, "The Influence of Literature and Myth in Videogames," *IGN*, May 18, 2006, http://www.ign.com/articles/2006/05/18/the-influence-of-literature-and-myth-in-videogames?page=3.

9. Anne C. Heller, *Ayn Rand and the World She Made* (New York: Doubleday, 2009), 195.
10. Heller, 92.
11. Ibid.
12. Andrew Ryan, "From the desk of Andrew Ryan," *Video*, Bathysphere Station.
13. IG. Admin, "From the Vault-The BioShock Pitch."
14. IG. Admin, "From the Vault-The BioShock Pitch."
15. Ibid.
16. Ibid.
17. Ibid.
18. Brendan Vance, "Ghosts of *BioShock*," *Brendan Vance* (blog), March 25, 2015, http://blog.brendanvance.com/2015/03/25/the-ghosts-of-bioshock/.
19. Critical Path, "CRITICAL PATH-Robin Hunicke-Games Are about Choice," *YouTube*, March 2, 2015, https://www.youtube.com/watch?v=dhZYQbEW0nM&list=WL&index=64.
20. Brigid Tenenbaum, *Dialogue*, Medical Pavilion.
21. *On-screen Instructions*, Medical Pavilion.
22. Ajar, "BioShock Spoiler Thread," *The Escapist* (forum), August 26, 2007, http://www.escapistmagazine.com/forums/read/9.48000-BioShock-Spoiler-Thread#318863.
23. Bonnie A. Nardi, *My Life as a Night Elf Priest: An Anthropological Account of World of Warcraft* (Ann Arbor, MI: University of Michigan Press, 2009), 137.
24. Nardi, 139.
25. Ajar, "BioShock Spoiler Thread."
26. Ibid.
27. Ibid.
28. Patricia Bayer, *Art Deco Architecture: Design, Decoration and detail from the twenties and thirties* (London: Thames and Hudson, 1992), 12.
29. David Garrard Lowe, *Art Deco New York* (New York: Watson-Guptill Publications, 2004) 8.
30. Heller, 113.
31. Bayer, 7–8.
32. IG. Admin, "From the Vault-The BioShock Pitch."
33. Heller, 46.
34. Heller, 235.
35. Irrational Games' Official Channel, "Rapture: A Modern Day Atlantis?," *YouTube*, October 4, 2013, https://www.youtube.com/watch?v=UsJDrsKNYxI.
36. Vossen, "Level design for melee combat systems."

37. Ibid.
38. Vossen, "Level design for melee combat systems."
39. Murray, 113.
40. Jack, *Narration*, Apollo Air Flight DF-0301.
41. Andrew Ryan, "A Man Chooses and a Slave Obeys," *Dialogue*, Rapture Central Control.
42. Rich Stanton, "Through The Looking Glass," *Rock, Paper, Shotgun*, March 26, 2014, http://www.rockpapershotgun.com/2014/11/26/bioshock-and-looking-glass/.
43. LeBlanc, 457.
44. Wesley Yin-Poole, "Levine: BioShock Infinite ending 'like nothing you've experienced in a video game before'," *Eurogamer*, December 18, 2012, http://www.eurogamer.net/articles/2012-12-18-levine-bioshock-infinite-ending-like-nothing-youve-experienced-in-a-video-game-before.
45. LeBlanc, 457.

CHAPTER 3

BioShock 2: Rapture Was Just the Beginning

Abstract Along with asking similar questions to the previous chapter, this chapter compares the two titles by means of hermeneutic horizons and franchise components.

Keywords Hermeneutic horizons • Franchise components • Collectivism • Nostalgia

Take-Two Interactive released *BioShock 2* on February 9, 2010.[1] Critically and financially, it was the least successful of the series. While *BioShock* received an aggregate Metacritic score of 95/100 and *BioShock Infinite* would go on to receive a 93/100, *BioShock 2* only garnered an 88/100.[2] Lainie Goldstein, Chief Financial Officer for Take-Two Interactive, was disappointed by *BioShock 2*'s performance in the marketplace, explaining that sales were "lower than expected… the title was well-received by the media and was profitable for us. However, sales slowed down sooner than we had expected."[3] *BioShock 2*'s Metacritic score and eventual gross revenue hardly warrant it regarded as a failure, but the game never grew out of the shadow of the original. Perhaps the cooler reception and sales was because the same core team behind the first *BioShock* and *BioShock Infinite* did not make *BioShock 2*. Instead of Ken Levine's Irrational Games developing the sequel, 2K Marin, a spinoff of the Boston-company located on

L. Reblin-Renshaw, *Ludonarrative Synchronicity in the 'BioShock' Trilogy*, https://doi.org/10.1007/978-3-030-63868-9_3

the opposite coast in Novato, California, made *BioShock 2*.[4] However, the change in crew also allowed *BioShock 2* the freedom to revise and re-work weak points found in the original *BioShock* such as the disillusionment of control and the lack of effect on player intrigue from dynamic choices.

The Beast of Ryan Lives

According to the *BioShock 2* website:

> Set approximately 10 years after the events of the original *BioShock*, the halls of Rapture once again echo with sins of the past. Along the Atlantic Coastline, a monster has been snatching little girls and bringing them back to the undersea city of Rapture. You are the very first Big Daddy as you travel through the decrepit and beautiful fallen city, chasing an unseen force in search of answers and your own survival.[5]

The player is placed in the role of Subject Delta who faces new foes, but also comes across some familiar faces. Brigid Tenenbaum, the "foster" mother for the Little Sisters explains to Subject Delta that he must reunite with Eleanor, the Little Sister he protected before her mother Sofia tried to kill him. Subject Delta's ties to Eleanor are so vital, that if he cannot find her, he will die. To survive Subject Delta must fight his way past members of The Rapture Family, followers of Sophia Lamb and her collectivism philosophy, along with Big Sisters, cyborgs who can go toe to toe to with Delta's mechanical weaponry.

BioShock 2 retains similar literary influences as its predecessor. Ayn Rand's *The Fountainhead* and *Atlas Shrugged* have little pertinence to the narrative of *BioShock 2*, but another work of hers is significant. Creative director Jordan Thomas featured her 1937 novella, *Anthem*, on his list of recommended reading for fans of *BioShock 2*.[6] The novella is set in a world without individuality, where the population has forgotten the word "I" and collectivism is the foundation for its society. *BioShock 2*'s villain, Sofia Lamb, promotes a group mentality that stands in stark contrast to Andrew Ryan's Objectivism. A combination of "John Stuart Mill, Karl Marx and other thinkers who promote the common good to the extreme, Lamb and her altruistic nature represents what Rand believed was the greatest problem of [the 20th] century:"[7] Or, as Andrew Ryan would say:

> What is the greatest lie every created? What is the most vicious obscenity ever perpetrated on mankind? Slavery? The Holocaust? Dictatorship? No.

> It's the tool with which all that wickedness is built: altruism. It is this great inversion, this ancient lie, which has chained humanity to an endless cycle of guilt and failure.[8]

"I would actually argue that most villains believe themselves to be altruists," says BioShock 2's creative developer Jordan Thomas.[9]

> Very few people consider themselves evil. The most extreme ideals in the whole of human cognition are typically behavior altering one; a system of restraint or a redistribution of power that is designed to uplift the species but usually ends up stamping out the rights of those people in question.[10]

Like Ryan, Lamb is "just another ideology given flesh," but Lamb's fanatical adherence to her beliefs is where the similarities end.[11] Her role in *BioShock 2* is less that of Andrew Ryan, but more along the line of Frank Fontaine. Lamb was a rival of Andrew Ryan and just as Fontaine took over when Jack killed Ryan, she takes over Rapture after Jack killed Frank. Eleanor is the final antagonist, but not the only villain featured in *BioShock 2*. Businessman and scientist Augustus Sinclair is also a combination of these two original *BioShock* characters. The size of his role, as a secondary villain whose death occurs approximately two/thirds through the game, parallels Andrew Ryan but personality wise he is the equivalent to Frank Fontaine: "a ruthless businessman who makes no secret of his plan to pick Rapture clean for profit."[12] Augustus Sinclair has the "self-awareness to know when it's time to drop the philosophy textbooks and have a human response to what fate has in store," and it is moments like that where "*BioShock 2* breaks away from being depressing… [and] speaks to an optimism that's often missing in Levine's characters."[13] *BioShock 2* does its best to avoid absolutes. Jordan Thomas, regarding the battle of minds between altruism/collectivism and Objectivism says, "the player will be exposed to far more philosophical viewpoints than these two extremes in *BioShock 2*."[14] Sinclair, who can be both of aid and an obstacle, represents moral relativism. Even the Big Daddy Subject Delta represents individualism that strays away from the intemperance of Ryan's Objectivism, for *BioShock 2* is "without the series' standard cynical view that everyone is just a scrap of power away from corruption. In *BioShock*, that extends to assuming the worst of the player for harvesting Little Sisters."[15]

The Big Daddies and Little Sisters play an integral role more pertinent than in the original *BioShock*. The sequel advances Brendan Vance's assertion that *BioShock* centered "on the crucial dynamic between Big Daddies and Little Sisters," and highlights their relationship to an even greater degree.[16] Not only do the player inhabit a Big Daddy in this iteration, but the game expands the mechanics and dynamics surrounding the Little Sisters as well. Before the option to harvest or rescue a Little Sister presents itself to Subject Delta, his first choice is to harvest or adopt the Little Sister. If the player chooses to adopt, then the Little Sister will search out for "angels," dead Splicers filled with ADAM. So instead of as in *BioShock*, where saving a Little Sister gave the player ADAM immediately, this time the player has to work to earn the reward. While a Little Sister is harvesting a corpse, the player must protect her from swarms of Splicers. If successful, the player will then have the original option: harvest or rescue. However, harvesting now gives the player even more ADAM than the initial harvest and the player has to fight off the new mini-boss, a Big Sister, after rescuing all the Little Sisters in a level. Just as Ajar performed a theorycrafting analysis for *BioShock*'s Little Sister moral quandary, a player by the handle system1021 analyzed the statistical complications presented in *BioShock 2*'s new harvesting system. Unlike its predecessor, it isn't nearly as clear whether it is better to harvest or rescue all the Little Sisters.

> Well, it actually comes out to a fairly even number either way. You initially get 80 less ADAM per sister if you save them, but after the 4th you get a tonic that reduces the gap to 40 less ADAM per sister. After 8 sisters you get another tonic that lets them harvest faster, which makes the onslaught of splicers a lot easier to deal with (though by this point they shouldn't be a huge issue for you). You also get about 350 ADAM from the presents the sisters leave you… Short answer is that by the end of the game it will be neck and neck for which one actually earns you more ADAM, with rescuing possibly winning out, but early game will be a lot easier if you harvest because you'll get the extra ADAM right away.[17]

In the first *BioShock*, it was statistically clear that the player would benefit more from rescuing the Little Sisters, thanks to the secondary benefits given to the player by Tenenbaum. However, in *BioShock 2*, dynamics heavily affect the difference between harvesting and adopting/rescuing. Player system1021 comments that it may be wise to assume that after dealing with eight Little Sisters the player has enough experience, has gained enough weapons and power-ups, to be able to handle the "onslaught of splicers a lot easier."System1021's recommendation that the "early game will be a lot easier if you harvest because you'll get the extra ADAM right away," goes to show that the decision is not nearly as cut and dry as in the first *BioShock*. The moral angle is still present in *BioShock 2*, but the player also must take into account a more multifaceted system of resource management and whether or not their skill level overrides a lack of resources. Just as the key NPCs with their more nuanced portrayals provide a more complex narrative than the original *BioShock*, the altered dynamic impacts of the Little Sister harvesting/adopting/rescuing mechanic complicating the moral dilemma.

BioShock 2's carry-over of such mechanics helps establish franchise components. According to Flint Dille and John Zuur Platten in their manual for writing and designing video games, franchise components are certain elements and qualities that make a game and its ilk unique.

> When story intersects, (you can decide whether it is a smooth merge or a collision) into the nitty-gritty of game design, this is where the larger franchise elements you develop for the property can really come into their own. Think about the unique ideas in your game, and how they could be expressed beyond gameplay and story.[18]

A franchise component should transcend narratology and ludology. These franchise components can also create horizons of expectations, ala Gadamer, for players familiar with previous titles. Collin Pointon, a philosopher and self-prescribed "slave to video games," applies Hans-George Gadamer's concepts to games saying that "players have a hermeneutic horizon that consists of conscious and unconscious ideas of what [a] game is, how it works, what to do in it, how it will affect them, what they want out of it, and so on".[19] These prejudices evolve over time, as players converse with the game, but their expectations also linger well after gameplay. This concept shares elements of nostalgia? According to Laurie N. Taylor and Zach Whalen, nostalgia can "be understood in constructive terms, as the process by which knowledge of the past is brought to bear on the present and the future".[20] The key difference here is, like ludonarrative *dissonance* versus ludonarrative synchronicity, is the connotation of the term constructive. To be nostalgic is to imagine a moment in the past positively. Hermeneutic horizons can produce a negative affect. Perhaps players were not a fan of the previous *BioShock* combat system. If this were the case, then alterations made to the mechanic would exceed, rather than fail to meet, expectations.

For the *BioShock* trilogy, the combat alternative of super-human power-ups sets the series apart from traditional FPS that focus on the use of range weapon and melee attacks alone. All three forms of combat remain in *BioShock 2*, with a few twists. The shooting mechanic retains the use of melee, range, and plasmid weaponry. There are several minor changes, such as the introduction of new types of guns and the reduction of several plasmids, but the major alteration comes with the dynamic of the shooting mechanic. The player now has "the ability to dual-wield weapons and plasmids, allow[ing] players to create exciting combinations of punishment."[21] Two narrative changes support this increase in combat power. First, the story takes place eight years after the original game. Though the city is under new management, it continually has to create and evolve new technologies. Secondly, the player's avatar is yet another science experiment: a Big Daddy. These cyborg creatures are deadly, dangerous, and deal a great deal of damage.

The Devil and the Deep Blue Sea

Critic Michael McWhertor felt that "*BioShock 2* does enough to differentiate itself from the original to make it feel new again, but it takes some time to get there."[22] Perhaps this lack of recognition to change is less a matter of the alterations being slow to appear and more a matter of the amount of time it took players to realize they were there all along. After a four-minute short film prologue, Subject Delta awakens in Adonis Luxury Resort, flooded, trashed, and with "Fallen, Fallen Is Babylon" graffiti etched out on the wall. Unlike the start of the first *BioShock*, in which the beauty and grandeur of Rapture awes Jack at first sight, in *BioShock 2* the player is immediately met with decay and destruction. The effects of having lost its founders eight years ago are immediately apparent. As Subject Delta traverses through Rapture, the city feels emptier than in the last game. The halls do not echo with the approach of Splicers. In *BioShock*, even before Jack climbed out of the bathysphere, he was attacked by a manic splicer. When Subject Delta wakes up in Adonis Luxury Resort, he isn't immediately pounced upon. He exits the room without consequence, pick up an item or two in the Adonis Baths and only then does he run into two splicers who are busy fighting each other, making them quick easy kills. Narratively, one can assume that the lack of enemies upfront is because the citizens, desperate for resources, have killed each other off. What the players will notice as they dive deeper into the game is that when a Splicer attacks Subject Delta, the enemy is never alone. These are Darwin's All-Stars; they have survived by banding together and being brutal. This change in behavior, their grouping up when attacking, is an influence by Sofia Lamb's Rapture Family, a religion based on her book, *Unity and Metamorphosis*. Followers of Lamb attack Subject Delta as per her orders and do so with great fervor, believing their actions just and in service to the greater good.

BioShock 2 altered the AI system for the Splicers. Not only are there more of them, but each of them is harder to kill than their *BioShock* counterparts. In *Kotaku*'s "Five Things Every Great First-Person Shooter Needs," GB Burford recommends worthy opponents.

> Enemies should be *tough* but also work to make you utilize the movement mechanics and the map you're in-in other words, enemies are about pushing you to use all the elements of the game. They're not fodder to be pointed and clicked on. They're environmental hazards to move you through the space in interesting ways.[23]

This increased level of difficulty is reflected by the change in mechanics and character design. Delta needs the ability to dual-wield weapons and plasmids in order to handle the onslaught of enemies. Narratively, this new amped up ability reflects the change in protagonist. As Jack "in *BioShock* you'd been a squishy man, but now you're an elite Big Daddy called Subject Delta, with a drill-arm capable of carving through splicers with impunity."[24]

BioShock 2 takes advantage of the new avatar by allowing players for the first time to explore the exterior of Rapture. With the use of his diving suit, Subject Delta can march along the ocean floor. This experience, viewing Rapture's skyscrapers and undiminished architecture from the outside, is one of only a few new visual moments of shock and awe that *BioShock 2* provides. These moments of underwater exploration provide a break from combat. They give the player an opportunity to appreciate the visual spectacle without fear of attack. While underwater combat would have been an interesting new mechanic with new dynamics impossible to perform in interior levels, the break from fighting does ease the tension and allows the terror affect not to overwhelm the player.

The level Ryan Amusements highlights all these adjustments, from the creation of larger, emptier levels as to accommodate more enemies to the increased level of brutality by both Splicers and Delta. Built by Carlson Fiddle, this theme park was meant to be "something magical, but instead [Ryan] turned it into a school… no, a cathedral. Dedicated to himself."[25] Now it lies in ruins, just like Ryan's dreams. The level is "a wonderful piece of design," piecing together what went wrong in between *BioShock* and *BioShock 2* "where dioramas depicting exactly the rules that would see Rapture turn from heaven to hell are depicted in fine style."[26] Ryan Amusements takes place at the end of the first third of *BioShock 2* and marks the transition from *BioShock* carbon copy to a game all its own. The level combines the tight corridors famous in *BioShock* with the large lobbies that are used for more than just boss fights in *BioShock 2*. This is also the first time the player meets a Little Sister in the game, learning of the new extended mechanic regarding the adoption option, and the first time a player must battle the game's new mini-boss, a Big Sister.

By the time the game reaches its climax, the changes in the level design from *BioShock* to *BioShock 2* are much more apparent. "Variation, not novelty, is the guiding aesthetic" and *BioShock 2* does this by having not only the narrative affected by choices made, but the level design as well.[27] The deaths, or lack thereof, by the player's accord, of three key NPCs (Poole, Holloway, and Alexander) is reflected in statues scattered throughout the last two levels of *BioShock 2*. Whether or not the player chooses to kill the NPCs alters the statues. A statue of the NPC Stanley Poole either shows Subject Delta extending his hand as a sign of mercy or using that hand to choke Poole. As Subject Delta accompanies a Little Sister through the penultimate level, Persephone, the monstrous child will point out all three artworks and make various comments depending on their merciful or brutal nature.

Here Comes the Bogeyman

As previously mentioned, the game opens with a four-minute short film prologue that establishes the character's backstory. Subject Delta is a first-generation Big Daddy and the first to properly bond with a Little Sister, who just happens to be Sofia Lamb's daughter. During the prologue, when a Splicer hits Subject Delta with a Hypnotize plasmid, Sofia commands the Big Daddy to kill himself. Ten years later, Eleanor Lamb awakens Delta. As the game continues, the player learn how she cared for

Subject Delta in secret for the past decade and now needs him to defeat her mother. The first image the player sees upon waking up is Subject Delta's reflection in the water. Both parts of this opening, the backstory and the reflection are two non-immersive elements that did not appear in *BioShock*. Also, while in the first *BioShock* there was a prologue in which the player was unable to control Jack's actions, this scene lasted under a minute. The opening of *BioShock 2* does not hand the controls over to the player for over four minutes. The absence of Subject Delta as a tabula rasa avatar, unlike Jack from *BioShock*, and the lack of agency for so long at the beginning of the game slows down the drive towards the creation of an immersive experience.

Though *BioShock 2* starts out less immersive than its predecessor does, the game does not feature the same "would you kindly" twist in the first *BioShock* that broke down the barrier between Jack's choices being that of the player's choice. Despite the presence of a Big Daddy's drill on the screen, the game seldom reminds the player what they are after this opening. Subject Delta's drill is also the reason for a change in the sequel's mechanics. In *BioShock*, Jack is not physically moving around pipes as he attempts to hack into various machinery. The act of hacking in the original *BioShock* is performed in a mini-game, which is a non-diegetic subgame featuring an entirely new set of mechanics and user interface. In *BioShock*, the mechanics for the hacking mini-game are based on the title, *Pipe Mania* (1989), in which Delta must rearrange segments of tubes into the correct pattern so that when the timer goes off, a liquid may flow through to the exit drain without resistance. While the mini-game lasts no longer than a minute or two, the abrupt change in point of view to an entirely new user-interface that is no longer in first-person perspective is a break in immersion. In *BioShock 2*, even if the pipe maneuvering were diegetic, Subject Delta would be unable to complete the task for he only possesses one gloved, bulky hand and a massive drill on his other arm. So instead, the sequel features a hacking system where the player must stop a needle on a specific colored portion of a gauge. This exercise could take place in the diegesis and therefore deepens the level of immersion.

Immersion is also aided by Subject Delta's free will, or to the degree that the player has free will upon the actions of Subject Delta. Jack's choices, for a majority of *BioShock*, were not his own and nor the players' either. According to creative director Jordan Thomas, the frustration Sofia Lamb expresses towards Subject Delta is that he "is the last individual in Rapture" and will not conform to the ideals of her Rapture Family.[28] Not only is this a major shift from the characterization of the protagonist in *BioShock*, but a rather large alteration to the idea of a Big Daddy in general. Their humanity was lost upon their mechanical transformation, and with it, any identification as human or individual. Subject Delta's journey towards individualism began after he lost himself to a Hypnotize plasmid. Upon waking, Subject Delta is a new man. Within the narrative, Subject Delta awakens to find that he no longer is bound by a majority of the brainwashing Big Daddies are subjected to. He is no longer required to protect the Little Sisters; he has free will. Outside of the diegesis, Subject Delta is a new man because instead of being controlled by his Big Daddy instincts, he is now being controlled by the player.

For Every Choice, There Is an Echo

Free will, as it pertains to immersion, is intertwined with its impact thematically as well. Choice is still a blatant theme in *BioShock 2*, just not the primary one. In comparison to the game's true thematic focus, individualism, choice is less a theme and more a function.

> So in celebrating the player's free will with the script this time, we have given more choices, such as whether to betray the Little Sisters' trust (which is something the other Big Daddys can't do) and what to do about the adult characters who are more challenging, ethically speaking. This aspect of free-will is both a key gameplay consideration as well as a device which helps push the plot forward.[29]

"Making various moral statements," such as deciding the fates of the Little Sisters and the three particular adult NPCs is what enables the developers to "learn a little bit more about [the player] and shape the outcome of the story" to an even greater extent than in *BioShock*.[30]

The choice to rescue, harvest, or adopt the Little Sisters is made even that much more difficult by the narrative. For those that played the first *BioShock*, the allegiance between a Big Daddy and their Little Sisters is a given notion. Even for players new to the *BioShock* universe, *BioShock 2*'s plot revolves around this deep connection between these mechanical monstrosities and their grossly genetically modified girls. Giving the players the option to harm a Little Sister is both free will for Subject Delta and the player. Armed with the knowledge of Subject Delta's backstory, the player can choose to act as they would expect Subject Delta to do so or as themselves. Unlike with playing as Jack, there is a clear distinction between players making choices by themselves or in line with the avatar's narrative. To some degree, this is more immersive than *BioShock* in which the players thought they were making their own decisions without Jack's influence since Jack was nothing more than an empty vessel through a majority of the game. With *BioShock 2*, the game does not remind the player whether a decision is theirs to make or one that the developers intended for them to choose, thus preserving the concept of a player-driven narrative.

In addition, unlike in *BioShock*, there are several other factors in deciding the narrative's conclusion. The Little Sisters are no longer the only NPCs whose fate affects the story. Choosing to kill or let live three side characters (Holloway, Poole and Alexander) alters the ending both narratively and visually as discussed earlier in the level design section. These choices drive home the theme of individualism not just because of what Subject Delta represents philosophically, but also because the decision to murder each of these characters is made on an individual-basis. The same goes for the Little Sisters. One can harvest one and then rescue another. However, the choice to end the life of Holloway, Poole, and Alexander relies on what the player knows of them as individuals and not a group identity as is the case for the Little Sisters.

Scattered throughout Rapture are optional audio diaries to listen to, providing some of the backstory for the NPCs, along with background information given to the player in real-time by Sofia Lamb and Augustus Sinclair.

> Through brilliant use of unreliable narrators and contradictory advice, these decisions can be truly difficult. We are left with our gun pointed at a quivering man or woman, at their most vulnerable. With the information at hand, are they worth being kept alive? We are given all the time we need to make our choice. Pull the trigger, or just walk out the door?[31]

While the choices in *BioShock* "amount[ed] to little more than doing what is morally the "right" thing to do or being a comic book style villain," the morality system in *BioShock 2* features a much more complex sense of mercy.[32]

The impetus for Subject Delta wanting to kill Stanley Poole is that, despite assisting the player in his fight against Sofia Lamb in game, Poole was the man who turned Subject Delta over to the authorities eight years ago and thus became a Big Daddy.

Grace Holloway does nothing but antagonize the player, even as Subject Delta looms over her, readying for the kill. Her hatred towards Delta, however, is misconstrued. Holloway loved Eleanor, but Sofia Lamb misled her in to thinking that Delta was behind her disappearance years back. The player is incapable of explaining him/herself and thus is left with the option to kill Holloway, who sent wave after wave of Rapture Family loyalists after Subject Delta or let her live despite the threat she poses even though she is not physically threatening. Over the radio Sinclair reminds the player that this is "your call, friend. Gracie's unarmed, for what it's worth."[33] Even if the player does not immediately shove a drill into her face, Gracie will continue to goad the player until he leaves her office.

This leads us to the greyest of morality choices in *BioShock 2*. Dr. Gilbert Alexander was a key scientist behind the creation of the Big Daddies and their bond with the Little Sisters. He is as much, if not more, to blame for Delta's current predicament as Poole. However, vengeance alone does not drive the decision whether to murder Alexander. Just as Delta finds Poole groveling and Holloway is too old to fight back, Alexander is in no condition to resist Delta physically. The player finds Dr. Alexander languishing away in a holding tank, his body mutated beyond recognition from too much ADAM. His mind too has mutated. Now going by the name "Alex the Great" now, Gilbert's consciousness can command security bots remotely to attack Delta and still maintains the ability to communicate.

After breaking Alexander's security system and obtaining the key for the next level, a recording from the "original" doctor plays.

> It is done, the sample disposal button on the panel in front of you will administer a massive jolt of electricity to the deck. More than enough to kill me. Whatever I might say to dissuade you, <u>do not listen</u>. The man whose voice you hear now is long gone. As my mind fades, I find my thoughts turn to the suffering that Eleanor will be made to endure. I am overcome with pity but I can only offer my feeble prayers. Perhaps after my death you could do more. Now, please, I ask you to grant me peace. Goodbye, my friend, and thank you.

This is not a direct address to Subject Delta. It is not like the screams of Alex the Great who begs and pleads for the player to ignore the death wish of his "old" self. Dr. Alexander wanted to die for what he done to Eleanor and her fellow Little Sisters and has been waiting for who knows how long to be released from his vile existence. The player must now decide whether he deserves to have his wish granted.

Summary

BioShock was not a game, narratively, clamoring for a sequel. Add in that *BioShock 2* was being produced by a sister studio and without the supervision of Ken Levine or any of the key crew members, the sequel faced an uphill battle from the start in regard to gaining acceptance from fans of the original and their horizons of expectations. While the sequel received praise for its re-worked mechanics and cleaner storytelling, it suffered from comparisons to its predecessor. *BioShock 2* is "a world less mysterious than when you last left it…[its] story does not have the same revelatory power or stunning, complete vision of the original. It is not as fresh or frightening."[34] While *BioShock 2* made the necessary changes to stand out from the original, those changes were not immediately clear enough to distance itself from its beloved predecessor. Echoing the reviews of several other critics, Richard Cobbet argued, "The basic chance to return to Rapture is more than worth your time on its own—assuming you're willing to give it an hour to find itself."[35]

BioShock 2 is what *BioShock* should have been, a game whose theme of choice and such consequences played out for the entirety of the game with its mechanics, dynamics, plot, and characters. While the narratological and ludological elements resemble to some degree *BioShock*, its ludonarrative synchronicity is more substantial. The choices players make regarding the killing (or not) of NPCs changes not only the narrative, but the level design as well. The game's nuanced plot and deeper characterization bleed into a more complex relationship with the avatar. Players retain free will to play Subject Delta as they please. Delta's background can influence their choices to kill certain characters or save others, information uncovered by listening to audio diaries can shape player's actions, or players can be merciless on their own accord. The game does not force players to make either decision and that is true to the theme of individualism and allows them to remain immersed in the game without it reminding them, like in *BioShock*, that their decisions are not of their own choosing.

This is not to say *BioShock 2* is without fault. While not a ludonarrative synchronicity issue, *BioShock 2* starts with a slow burn for its first act, though this is far less a sin than *BioShock*'s late game deviation with its own mid-point twist in theme. *BioShock 2* still maintains the multiple ending possibilities that caught the attention of critics and players alike with the original *BioShock* and does so without contradicting itself. However, *BioShock 2* was placed in the dubious position where good wouldn't be good enough. The game needed to be just as revolutionary to overcome the horizons of expectations set by players of the original. Due to rapid canonization of *BioShock*, it should not have come as a surprise to 2K games that *BioShock 2* was not met with the same level of adulation.

Notes

1. Take-Two Interactive is the parent company of 2K Games.
2. Metacritic is a site that gathers multiple reviews and produces an aggregate score, one based on critics' ratings and another based on player submitted scores. The numbers presented here are based on the critic's ratings and are the average of each game between the three consoles they appeared on.
3. Ludwig Kietzmann, "Take-Two Q2 revenue up to $268M, BioShock 2 sales 'lower than expected'," *Endgadget*, June 8, 2010, http://www.engadget.com/2010/06/08/take-two-q2-revenue-up-to-268-million-bioshock-2-sales-low/.
4. Marin County is also home to another video game studio with a focus on narrative-based products: Telltale Games, Inc.
5. "Story," *BioShock 2*, www.BioShock2game.com/en/.
6. Nick Cowen, "BioShock 2 developer interview," *The Telegraph*, January 13, 2010, http://www.telegraph.co.uk/technology/video-games/6980675/BioShock-2-developer-interview.html.
7. Heller, 91.
8. Andrew Ryan, "Speech," *Public Address*, Medical Pavilion.
9. Thomas was also the level designer for Fort Frolic in the first *BioShock*.
10. Cowen, "BioShock 2 developer interview."
11. Richard Cobbett, "BioShock 2 retrospective," *Eurogamer*, July, 4, 2013, http://www.eurogamer.net/articles/2013-04-07-bioshock-2-retrospective.
12. Cobbett, "BioShock 2 retrospective."
13. Ibid.
14. Cowen, "BioShock 2 developer interview."
15. Cobbett, "BioShock 2 retrospective."
16. Vance, "Ghost of BioShock."
17. system1021, "Should I rescue or harvest little sisters?" *GameFAQs*, 2010, http://www.gamefaqs.com/xbox360/945380-bioshock-2/answers/165562-should-i-rescue-or-harvest-little-sisters.
18. Flint Dilly and John Zuur Platten, *The Ultimate Guide to Video Game Writing and Design* (Los Angeles: Lone Eagle Publishing Company, 2007), 111.

19. Collin Pointon, "BioShock's Meta-Narrative," *BioShock and Philosophy: Irrational Game, Rational Book* (West Sussex: Wiley Blackwell, 2015), 7–8.
20. Whalen, 3.
21. "Information," *BioShock 2*, www.BioShock2game.com/en/.
22. McWhertor, "BioShock 2 Review: In Case of Rapture."
23. GB Burford, "Five Things Every Great First-Person Shooter Needs," *Kotaku*, October, 31, 2014, http://kotaku.com/five-things-every-great-first-person-shooter-needs-1653281844.
24. Cobbett, "BioShock 2 retrospective."
25. Carlson Fiddle, "The Old Sheepdog," *Audio Diaries*, Ryan Amusements.
26. Cobbett, "BioShock 2 retrospective."
27. Alec Meer, "Wot I Think: Bioshock 2," *Rock, Paper, Shotgun*, February 8, 2010, http://www.rockpapershotgun.com/2010/02/08/wot-i-think-bioshock-2/.
28. Cowen, "BioShock 2 developer interview."
29. Ibid.
30. Ibid.
31. Daniel Carbone, "Death and Ethical Violence," *Kotaku*, April 29, 2010, http://kotaku.com/5527216/death-and-ethical-violence.
32. Ibid.
33. Augustus Sinclair, *Dialogue*, Pauper's Drop.
34. Michael McWhertor, "BioShock 2 Review: In Case Of Rapture," *Kotaku*, February 8, 2010, http://kotaku.com/5466745/bioshock-2-review-in-case-of-rapture.
35. Cobbett, "BioShock 2 retrospective."

CHAPTER 4

BioShock Infinite: The New Eden

Abstract The final case study explores the most distinct title of the franchise and how a game with such different content and tropes can still manage to feature enough key components and questions to below in the trilogy.

Keywords Violence • Fallacy • Columbia • Genre • Agency

A week after Irrational Games officially announced that they were indeed working on a new *BioShock* title, a trailer for *Infinite* was featured at Gamescom 2010, the "world's largest trade fair and event highlight for interactive games and entertainment."[1] The trailer made it immediately clear that *Infinite* would be a grand departure for the *BioShock* franchise. The Gamescom Demo Gameplay Footage opens in first-person, but even before the viewer sees a disembodied hand of the protagonist, a voice is heard. For the first time in *BioShock* history, the main avatar speaks! As the un-named character walks up a cobblestone street, it becomes clearer that the lighting from above is not artificial, but natural sunlight. Rather than a city underwater, *Infinite* takes place on a city in the air. The rest of the footage shows more proto-typical *BioShock* gameplay: overpowered weaponry, violent citizenry, mechanical monstrosities, and otherworldly

L. Reblin-Renshaw, *Ludonarrative Synchronicity in the 'BioShock' Trilogy*, https://doi.org/10.1007/978-3-030-63868-9_4

power-ups. The combat shown is gory and gruesome, but also takes place in larger, open areas than its predecessors.

In the span of seven days, *Infinite* went from being completely unknown to IGN's Game of the Show.[2] In the two and a half years before the game's release on March 26, 2013, *BioShock Infinite* was nominated for over and won nearly a hundred awards, including three consecutive "Most Anticipated Game" for Spike's Video Game Awards and nominations in both 2011 and 2012 for "One to Watch" at the Golden Joystick Awards.[3] When *Infinite* finally hit the market, it did so triumphantly, living up to the hype by outselling both its predecessors and receiving far better reviews than *BioShock 2*.

Where *BioShock 2* faced an uphill battle against the horizons of expectations associated with the original *BioShock*, *Infinite* had to overcome franchise expectations and changes to the FPS landscape. Since the release of *BioShock 2* in 2010, numerous FPS titles had been released that were meta-commentaries of the genre. *Call of Duty: Modern Warfare 2* (2009) featured a controversial mission referred to as "No Russian." Just as Jack/the player in *BioShock* was forced to murder Andrew Ryan against his will, in this *Call of Duty* the player is embedded in a Russian terrorist group and becomes embroiled in an airport massacre. While not required to shoot the unarmed civilians, the player cannot stop the atrocities from happening either. *Far Cry 3* (2012) also uses ultra-violence to highlight players over-exposure to such sensationalism. In an interview with PC gaming site *Rock, Paper, Shotgun*, writer Jeffrey Yohalem wanted to "make a game that [was] a warning label about games." Rather than maintain the illusion of immersion, the game "constantly jolts [players] out of the narrative system… directing attention towards the systems."[4] *Infinite* needed to find a way to players willingly participate in violent confrontations, even when their hermeneutic horizons towards such brutality was beginning to waver.

Bring Us the Girl, and Wipe Away the Debt

The official *BioShock Infinite* website provides the following plot summary:

> Set in 1912… former Pinkerton agent Booker DeWitt [is] sent to the flying city of Columbia on a rescue mission. His target? Elizabeth, imprisoned since childhood by the city's founder, Zachary Hale Comstock. During their daring escape, Booker and Elizabeth form a powerful bond—one that lets Booker augment his own abilities with her world-altering control over

> the environment. Together, they fight from high-speed Sky-Lines, in the streets and houses of Columbia, on giant zeppelins, and in the clouds, all while learning to harness an expanding arsenal of weapons and abilities.[5]

Along the way, Booker and Elizabeth become embroiled in the civil unrest brewing in Columbia. The Vox Populi, led by Daisy Fitzroy, challenge the elite citizenry and their eschewing of Christian and Founding Father values that have created a society of discrimination and neo-capitalism run amuck. But can Booker and Elizabeth trust the rebellion in helping their escape or are the anarchists just another violent cult out for their own means?

No longer were Ken Levine and Irrational Games dependent upon Ayn Rand to provide the foundation for their narrative. A FPS sprinkled with sci-fi elements may seem an unlikely benefactor of a historical novel's influence, however *BioShock Infinite* owes much of its storyline to Erik Larson's *The Devil in the White City: Murder, Magic, and Madness at the Fair That Changed America*. This non-fiction novel follows two men of great importance to the Chicago World Fair of 1893, also known as the World's Columbian Exposition. Daniel H. Burnham was the Director of Works for the fair, while Dr. H. H. Holmes was a serial killer who took advantage of the influx of fresh targets brought to town by the fair. There are several, even if loose, connections between these historical figures and those of *Infinite*'s main "protagonist" and "antagonist."[6] Like Burnham, Comstock was the impetus behind the creation of his Columbia, a feature at the Chicago World Fair back in 1893 within the fictional timeline of *BioShock*. Like Holmes, Booker does bring death and destruction upon Comstock's city.[7]

While Comstock and Booker have their historical counterparts in our reality, they have parallels in the fiction of Rapture as well. Zachary Hale Comstock is *Infinite*'s Andrew Ryan, both founder and tyrant.[8] He is also like Sofia Lamb, a religious zealot who does not take kindly to non-believers. Anarchist (or revolutionist, depending on your financial status in Columbia) Daisy Fitzroy shares a similar function as that of Atlas in the original *BioShock*. While she appears to make a fair trade with Booker helping her and in return she provides he and Elizabeth the means of escape, Fitzroy is only using Booker, so she can overtake Comstock's rule. The parallels continue with all three *BioShock* games featuring a businessman who follows his own rules of Social Darwinism rather than the teachings of their leader, whether this be Frank Fontaine, Augustus Sinclair, or Jeremiah Fink in *Infinite*.

What makes the third *BioShock* title unique is the lack of direct parallels for its narratological components to the prior *BioShock* games. The settings, from a dystopia under the sea to a utopia in the sky, are as diametric opposites as can be designed. The story tries to jam together *BioShock* and *BioShock 2*'s narrative into a swashbuckling adventure to both save the girl and escape the city, resulting in an over-burdened plot. There are no Splicers or Big Sisters. There are no Big Daddies or Little Sisters. Instead, *Infinite* gives us the Lutece Twins, a pair of siblings whose main functions appear to be spouting riddles and have no narratological or ludological counterpart in either *BioShock* or *BioShock 2*. Unlike *BioShock 2*, with its emphasis on variation by extension, *Infinite* alters both the ludology and narratology often with reduction. Without the presence of the Little Sisters, the entire mechanic of harvesting or rescuing is eliminated. Hacking is also absent from *Infinite* which leaves shooting as the only mechanic, outside of basic movement, to be featured in all three games.[9] The player still has the option to shoot with weapons or use superhuman powers. In *BioShock* and *BioShock 2*, plasmids were a key element tied to both the setting and plot. Rapture, in part, fell due to the over-use of plasmids by its citizenry. They were a creation of the free-market Andrew Ryan instilled and his emphasis on unchecked scientific research. In the world of Columbia, these abilities are named vigors rather than plasmids. Vigors are marketed and sold to the public ala a carnival sequence at the beginning of the game, where the citizenry can try out items like Possession or Bucking Bronco. This, however, is the last time Booker encounters civilian playing with vigors. Rather than facing "tweaked-out" Splicers, Booker faces off against experienced enforcers, such as the Crow and Fireman, who have mastered these abilities. Vigors are more useful to Booker and his combat dynamics in *Infinite*, rather than a dependency on the powerful weaponry at hand. In *BioShock*, a core dynamic was combining the plasmids with specific weapons, like freezing opponents with Winter Blast and then smashing them into ice cubes with a wrench. In *BioShock 2*, the player could dual-wield plasmids and weapons for more brutal attacks. *Infinite*'s fighting style centers around vigor combinations, like using Murder of Crows (conjures a swarm/murder of vicious crows) followed by Devil's Kiss (flame-based projectile) to create a fiery birdemic. The reduction of vigors available to the player also exemplifies the focus to combining vigor powers as the new key dynamic. *Infinite* features fewer vigor options than either *BioShock* or *BioShock 2* and the player is only capable of equipping two vigors at a time rather than allowing the player to cycle through all the vigors they have earned. In the first two *BioShock* titles, the player could choose from all the plasmids they collected by way of a plasmid wheel, a set of gears that appeared onscreen that players could then rotate through until they found the power they wanted to use for a situation. Players also had the option of rotating through all of their plasmids without the visual assistance of the plasmid wheel. In *BioShock Infinite* the plasmid (or vigors in this case) wheel has been removed. Players can only cycle through two vigors in real-time. If players wish to substitute out one of these vigors, then they must pause the game and replace one or both vigor slots with a new choice of superpower. This change creates more difficult battle scenarios and changes the pace of the game, with players having to spend extra time setting up their game plan by choice of vigors before jumping into a battle. The alteration to the series franchise component was just one of numerous changes to the combat portion of *Infinite* and contributed to more complex but also more challenging scenarios. Many more of those changes spawned from the new level design.

A City Lighter than Air

Visually, *Infinite* starts as that of its two predecessors. Just as Jack's plane crashes into the ocean, like Subject Delta awakening to see his reflection in a puddle, Booker DeWitt's story begins in the water. An unknown man and woman row him to a lighthouse, not the same as the one Jack found in the Atlantic but a lighthouse nonetheless. This time, however, when Booker DeWitt enters, instead of diving deep into the ocean, a rocket launches him high into the sky.

Booker lands in the Church of Comstock, a space that has remnants of the Art Deco architecture previously seen in Rapture. Booker wades through water as what at first are dark hallowed halls begin to glow from candlelight. The Church of Comstock has similar aesthetic qualities to the Art Deco church designs of New York such as the use of stained glass and gold similar to those featured in St. Andrew Avellino Church.[10] Religious structures of the period commonly featured elements from other forms or architecture, such as combining Art Deco and the Gothic Revival style.[11] The 1926 Liberty Memorial in Kansas City, Missouri had both a "Neoclassical bent [and] contained Art Deco elements." Inside the

Church of Comstock, players can also find several neoclassical statues of figures such as Lady Comstock and Elizabeth. The Château Thierry in Bellicourt, France was also an Art Deco hybrid with a "Neoclassical temple form guarded by a massive stylized eagle behind a symbolic render of the Stars and Stripes."[12] The Church of Comstock features multiple patriotic imagery combined with religious symbolism, a trend that continues upon entering Columbia.

Before the player may enter the city, they require a baptism. Booker approaches a golden, metallic wrought archway One need look no further than Louis Sullivan, one of the influential architects for Ayn Rand's *The Fountainhead*, to find the inspiration for this transport into Columbia. Louis Sullivan's design of the Transportation Building for the World's Columbian Exposition was a major departure from the classical style of the other Great Buildings: The building's main entrance was an immense single arch known as the 'Golden Doorway.' The doorway was stunning in its intricate metal design. This grand portal featured a series of receding arches entirely overlaid in gold leaf.[13] Architecture and level design, particularly the propylaeum, transition the player from the familiar world of *BioShock* toward an entirely new interpretation of the series. The World's Columbian Exposition is the main influence for the level design of Comstock's utopia. The name of the fair was reference to the quadricentennial of Columbus' discovery of America. After the success of the International Exposition of 1889 in Paris, the planners behind the Chicago World's Fair were "challenged, not only to equal, but to surpass what the French had accomplished."[14] The event was a spectacle of American Exceptionalism. Comstock modeled his city on not only its architecture, but also its purpose as well. Henry Van Brunt, one of the members of the Commission of Architects, explained that "what was to be found at the exposition was not architecture in its highest sense, but rather a scenic display, composed—to use a theatrical term—of 'practicable' models, executed on a colossal stage."[15] Nicknamed the White City, the ultimate purpose was for the fair to be an ideal for other American cities.[16] Comstock took the colossal portion literally, along with a few of the cities' "darker" aspects. While the nickname White City came from its color palettes, the Columbian Exposition also faced troubles with Native American groups and other minorities.[17] The fair presented Asians of multiple descents in various exhibits as nothing more than inaccurate stereotypes.

The level Soldier's Field features the Hall of Heroes, a sequence that parallels Ryan Amusements in *BioShock 2* for its mixture of tight halls lined with dioramas but also larger, emptier levels as to accommodate more brutal enemies. Here Booker and Elizabeth find two racist diorama displays. The first is a representation of the Boxer Rebellion, a historical event that in the fictional universe of *BioShock* Columbia used its capabilities as an aerial craft of war to decimate the Chinese. The second display is that of another historical event, the Wounded Knee Massacre, in which Booker took part in the *BioShock*'s diegesis. Just as Ryan Amusements shows the history of Rapture and its eventual downfall, the Hall of Heroes does much the same. The player does not know until the conclusion of *BioShock Infinite* that Booker's guilt over his part during the Battle of Wounded Knee led him to find God and change his identity to Zachary Hale Comstock. But thanks to the parallel universe theory integral to *Infinite*' plot and gameplay, Booker's action at Wounded Knee made him a great soldier and provided the skills necessary for the non-Comstock version to destroy Columbia.

Despite the cultural ugliness of the Hall of Heroes, a good portion of *BioShock Infinite* is built around being aesthetically pleasing to the eye. Steve Anichini, principal graphics programmer for *BioShock Infinite* explains:

> The size of the levels were bigger than anything Irrational had attempted before... this meant much bigger and much more open spaces that still retained the high detail required for environmental storytelling, because much of the story telling in a *BioShock* game was done via the world itself.[18]

While a player can explore the grandeur that is Columbia, absorbing all its detail and appreciating the result of more powerful graphics, the splendor of the city does not make up for its lack of genre appropriateness. *BioShock Infinite*'s story is that of a rescue (or escort) mission. Booker DeWitt attempts to sneak into Columbia, go unnoticed, find Elizabeth, and sneak her away without causing a fuss. This plot lends itself more towards the stealth genre than it does a FPS. There are stealth games told in the first-person perspective such as *Thief* (1998) and *Dishonored* (2012). These titles allow the player to guide the avatar in attempts to traverse unnoticed, but they do not feature the scale of combat or similar weaponry found in *BioShock Infinite*. The trials and tribulations Booker and Elizabeth face as they try to escape Columbia undetected is a story best fit for the third-person stealth genre rather than a FPS like *BioShock Infinite*. Third-person stealth games, such as *Metal Gear Solid 2: Sons of Liberty* (2001), are known for their escort missions. *BioShock 2* did have its moments in which the player could perform an escort mission, protecting a Little Sister as she gathered ADAM. However, there are two differences between *BioShock 2*'s escort function and *Infinite*. First, *BioShock* 2's missions were optional and not the focus of the entire game, unlike *BioShock Infinite*'s narrative. Secondly, *BioShock 2*'s level design was built to accommodate the protection of young, female non-playable character (NPC). *Infinite*'s level design was simply not developed with this dynamic in mind.

Instead, as is in many FPSs, the level design for *Infinite* centers on combat, the very task Booker is attempting to avoid. The design of Columbia features numerous wide, open spaces. These areas accommodate many enemies and the developers always take advantage of this.

> The original *BioShock*'s Rapture was a dark, claustrophobic place full of corridors and rooms that accommodated only small-scale battles. *BioShock Infinite*'s Columbia, with its massive floating city blocks, allows for a much wider range of tactics and behaviors. Enemies can be engaged both in close combat and with long-range weapons across huge expanses–and everywhere in between. But they will also take advantage of the same opportunities you have, as they work together and zip around on Sky-Lines to outflank and outwit you.[19]

Why is Booker forced to participate in such large-scale carnage? It does not serve a plot where an outsider attempts to steal away a princess of sorts from a possessive and paranoid city prone to violence.

Both Sinner and Saint

Unlike the previous *BioShock* avatars, players know nearly everything about Booker DeWitt: what he looks like, his birthday, details of his past, and even what he sounds like. Booker is the first *BioShock* protagonist that speaks, apart from Jack's opening monologue. Voice actor Troy Baker has pages upon pages of dialogue, interacting with a majority of the *Infinite* cast. Booker talks as he observes his surroundings, cries for help during combat, and chews the fat during *Infinite*'s many cut scenes. Returning to Robin Hunicke's view on choice, "games can be about empowering you to see and experience someone else's perspective."[20] This is how *Infinite* differs greatly from the previous two *BioShocks*. The player is Booker DeWitt; he is not them.

However, it is not just the altered nature of the game's avatar that breaks the immersive nature the series has thus far strived to create. *Infinite* features a basic mechanic of many FPS that inevitably pulls the player out of the game. Rich, in the episode "Why Mario is more Immersive than Call of Duty" from the web series *Previously Recorded*, proposes that for horror "you need to be immersed, you need to be there."[21] The video references the recent *Call of Duty: Advance Warfare* (2014) in which the player attends the funeral service of a fellow soldier and friend, only to be asked to "press X" in order to pay their respects. Rich argued that the mechanic of button prompts, instructions that tell the player exactly what they are supposed to do specifically, break immersion in a game regardless of genre. These instructions are addressing the player, not their avatar. *BioShock* and *BioShock 2* featured several button prompts, but they typically were for simple tasks like "open door" or "pull lever." Button prompts used for complex actions such as "jump ledge" or "swing across room" take away agency and sensory feedback, removing the challenge affect and limiting dynamic options for players. *Infinite* featured far more promptings to tap X, including an instance that spurred religious controversy. Only minutes into the game, the player is asked to press a button in order to be baptized and thus enter Columbia, a city based on religious zealotry. If the player chooses not to be baptized, they cannot continue with the game. At this early point in *Infinite*, the player is not fully Booker. *Infinite*'s opening retains much of that visual style and narrative similarities of the previous two *BioShock* games. This leads the player, due to horizons of expectations, to assume that the level immersion in *Infinite*, where they are making choices as their own not just as the character, will continue. Gamer Green Malmberg felt that being forced to perform this action of baptism was an affront to his religion and requested (and received) a full refund from Valve, an online video game distributor, for his purchase of *Infinite*.[22] Twitter responses to *Kotaku*'s article on the subject proved that even though the choice "felt ham-handed," many believe it was a decision not meant to be made by the player's own ethics. "I'm not being me," said one respondent, "I'm Booker DeWitt. Booker DeWitt don't give a shit." Up until this point, Booker's dialogue has been sparse and even Jack had a few words to say at the beginning of *BioShock*. Having a decision such as this early on the game, where developer's insistence drives the plot so heavily and leaves no choice for the player, is where the game clearly breaks away from its predecessors regarding immersion.

Perhaps the over-use and controversial button prompts in *Infinite* spawn from the fact that this game does not feature a horror affect, unlike the previous two. The level of immersion required to create this mood is not as necessary for a game that does not desire the player to be scared. There are, however, moments of desire to X out of a situation that is conspicuously missing from *Infinite*. The game features around an hour worth of cutscenes that, while the player is still able to control the camera, they are robbed of the option to skip these conversations. While the exposition provided during these interludes can be integral to the plot development, they do hamper both replay value and flow. Montage-free cinematic interludes such as these, as discussed by Alexander Galloway in "Origins of the First-Person Shooter" are meant to make gameplay fluid and continuous.[23] Providing a false sense of control achieves the opposite effect, an affect of frustration and annoyance, another-imposed pause.

After an intense and lengthy battle sequence, rather than building upon this kinetic energy, the game often slows down or even halts progress for a moment of reflection. The pacing of the game is out of the hands of the player, overtly manipulated by the designers. One of the appeals of the earlier *BioShock* titles was the covert influence of the developers upon the telling of the narrative. Both *BioShock* and its sequel would present supplementary narrative information by means of audio diaries that players had the option of listening to. *Infinite* features similar Voxophones, but they are not as frequently placed throughout the levels. While these recordings play, players have the freedom to move about levels and aren't restricted in where to go or how to advance, unlike during *Infinite*'s cutscenes. Even orders given by Atlas in *BioShock* were placed at moments that allowed the player the ability to continue their missions simultaneously. While there were a handful of sequences that placed greater restrictions on the player in the earlier *BioShocks*, their infrequency only heightened the significance of their loss of control.

A Choice Is Better than None

BioShock Infinite does not feature the Big Daddy/Little Sister moral quandary that the first two *BioShock* games revolved around. There are, however, still ethical questions revolving around violence. Unlike in Rapture, where behind every corner is the potential for a Splicer ready to cut your head off, the citizens of Columbia are not out for blood… at least not without warrant. "Her citizens have more unpredictable motives, and their enmity—or their loyalty—can't be taken for granted," which is why once a Columbian has been provoked; the player must be ready to fight them and their loyal brethren.[24] Killing a Splicer in Rapture was a matter of survival, kill or be killed. Murdering citizens of Columbia is less cut and dry. ADAM drove rapture dwellers mad, devolved them, and thus killing them was almost mercy. Those in Columbia attack Booker out of fear, and rather than give the player the option to run away and hide or even incapacitate rather than cause lethal damage, the player more often must kill not just officers of the law but also simple bar patrons and wrong place-wrong time crowd members.

Choice is still relevant, but in the case of *BioShock Infinite*, the theme is about the futility of choice. However, this theme is unclear until the end of the game's narrative when the plot reveals the nullification of players' choices throughout the franchise. During the first playthrough, players are unaware that their intrigue-oriented actions are futile. The actions of Booker DeWitt/the player inevitably escalate into violence, whether he chooses heads or tails. For instance, when Booker arrives in Raffle Plaza, he is chosen to participate in a sadistic, racist ritual: throwing a baseball at an interracial couple. The player does not have to throw the ball at them. The player can peg the host of the raffle, Jeremiah Fink, instead for leading such a despicable display. Alternatively, they can even refuse to throw period. However, no matter what the player chooses, the result will be the same. A member of the crowd will notice the "mark of the False Shepherd" upon Booker's hand and the police arrive. Later, when Booker and Elizabeth attempt to gain passage out of town, Booker's inability to keep a low profile comes back to haunt him. When he approaches the ticket booth, Booker overhears the clerks call for backup. He has two choices now: pull out a weapon or sternly ask for the tickets. Either way, Booker ends up yet again surrounded and forced to fight off wave after wave of angry citizens and police officers. Not only are the consequences for Booker's choice inevitable, but optional moments of violence in the game are without consequence at all. When security is not around, Book can randomly kill civilians. There is a reaction, the quick cry of agony and viscera exploding from their heads, but Booker is rewarded for his behavior, not punished. Killing innocents is too often necessary to steal resources off their dead bodies. Lacking the hacking mechanic, which lowered the cost of items in *BioShock* and *BioShock 2*, or the gifts from the Little Sisters, makes managing money and vigors that much more difficult in *Infinite*.

The Lutece Twins, who all too often confuse Booker by speaking in the future tense, provide hints towards the game's theme and its parallel universe theory. At Monument Island, Robert and Rosalind Lutece approach Booker. Robert wears a chalkboard around his neck with two columns: heads and tails. The former features thirteen tallies, the latter has none. "Heads or tails," they ask. Booker flips the coin. It's heads. "I never find that as satisfying as I'd imagine," says Robert. "Chin up, there's always next time," responds Rosalind. "I suppose there is."[25] Robert turns around, revealing another chalkboard with the entire heads column filled with tallies. This scene, and its awkward use of grammar, is the result of Booker having met the Lutece Twins multiple times before during his numerous failed attempts to rescue Elizabeth, not that he (or the player) remembers or knows any of this at this point in the game.

The multiple endings featured in *BioShock*, the reveal that the player's choices somewhat mattered, was a major twist for storytelling in the FPS genre. For *BioShock 2*, due to pre-established hermeneutic horizons, varied endings were to be expected. The twist with *Infinite* was that there was no twist. The third *BioShock* chose not to have the player's decisions alter the game's conclusion. The lengthy epilogue for *Infinite*, in which the player no longer complete any combat missions but instead is only capable of moving Booker around and having him perform simple tasks like opening doors and pressing buttons, reveals how the game retconned the entire series. As previously discussed, Comstock and DeWitt are one in the same, merely different versions of the same man from different parallel universes. Elizabeth can access these universes through "tears," and it is these tears that connect Rapture to Columbia. The vigors that seem out of place in *Infinite*? Those were plasmids acquired by Jeremiah Fink after an interdimensional trip to Rapture. The monstrous man-machine hybrids known as the Big Daddies? Those were the basis for Elizabeth's mechanical guardian, Songbird. Before the final scene, in which multiple versions of Elizabeth from multiple universes kill Booker prior to his baptism and transformation into Comstock, Elizabeth reveals an endless sea of infinite lighthouses. "There's always a city, a man, and a lighthouse," she says.[26] Whatever decision made, whether it be in *BioShock*, *BioShock 2*, or *BioShock Infinite*, is played out simultaneously in some other lighthouse, in a way eliminating the significance of all choices players made throughout the entirety of the series. Even if players played Jack as a moral man, somewhere else he was harvesting all those Little Sisters. Ryan, Fontaine, and the player were not the only puppeteers; fate is the ultimate developer.

Summary

This reveal greatly alters the game's instances of ludonarrative synchronicity. Up until the epilogue, *Infinite* seems to faulter with all three elements of analysis: theme, level design, and immersion. It is only after an initial playthrough that aspects of the level design and thematic focus on irrational violence appear ludonarratively synced.

The level design works for and against the game's narrative. As a representative of theme, the level design is ludonarratively synced. The architecture with its use of balanced, mirrored levels, where going left or right is irrelevant, foreshadows the game's irrelevancy of choice as a theme. Regarding combat and narrative, the level design fails (at first) to be ludonarratively synced. Instead of providing Booker with an environment in which he could hide and sneak by enemies to help Elizabeth escape, as would be expected for a stealth story and escort missions, *Infinite* is designed as a stereotypical FPS and builds its levels to be brutal warzones. Again, it isn't until the game is replayed that this failure is given reason. It is not noticeable during the first playthrough, but Elizabeth cannot be hurt. Unlike the Little Sisters in *BioShock 2* that need protection, Elizabeth is assisting Booker survive. Booker's inability to avoid confrontation, forced to fight, is another example of lack of choice. The restriction to the combat dynamics, less vigors and limited use of them, also foreshadows the theme of choice as a farce. There are other hints, presented mainly through the Lutece Twins, that choice is unobtainable. Again, these moments of ludonarrative synchronicity are only made apparent at the completion of the game.

One issue the epilogue reveal cannot solve is the low level of immersion. *Infinite*'s greatest struggle by ludonarrative synchronicity standards is its failure to maintain immersion. There are the long, unskippable conversations in which Elizabeth converses with Booker, looking directly at the screen and breaking the fourth wall. Too many times the game reminds the player that it is just a game by featuring multiple quick-time events rather than allowing the player the agency to perform complex tasks themselves. While the diegetic form of immersion is broken, the non-diegetic example of player-avatar relations does remain steady. The answer to the fourth dramatic inquiry question "does the game start (with the predefined narrative) and end (through the player's intrigue-oriented ergodic log") with the same avatar-player relationship," is yes. They just don't play the game knowing this.

Notes

1. Federal Association of Interactive Entertainment Software, http://www.gamescom-cologne.com/en/gamescom/home/index.php.
2. Martin Robinson, "Gamescom: BioShock Infinite Wins Game of Show," *IGN*, August 20, 2010, http://www.ign.com/articles/2010/08/20/gamescom-bioshock-infinite-wins-game-of-show.
3. *BioShock Infinite*, http://www.bioshockinfinite.com/the-game.
4. Nathan Grayson, "Fire Away: Spec Ops, Far Cry 3 Writers on Criticizing FPS," *Rock Paper Shotgun*, April 9th, 2013, https://www.rockpapershotgun.com/2013/04/09/fire-away-spec-ops-far-cry-3-writers-on-criticizing-fps/.
5. *Synopsis*, http://www.BioShockInfinite.com/the-game/.
6. As spoiled by the end of the game, Booker DeWitt and Zachary Hale Comstock is the same person, just from alternate universes. Therefore DeWitt/Comstock is both protagonist and antagonist, hence the use of quotations.
7. Booker is technically a spree killer rather than a serial killer, regardless of a similar death toll.
8. He is also Ryan's worst nightmare, the sort of religious zealot he felt destroyed America and led him underwater.
9. Basic movement includes walking, jumping, crouching, etc.
10. Carla Breeze, *American Art Deco: Architecture and Regionalism* (New York: W.W. Norton & Company, 2003), 55.
11. Bayer, 196.
12. Ibid.
13. Normon Bolotin and Christine Laing, *The World Columbian Exposition: The Chicago World's Fair of 1893* (Chicago: University of Illinois Press, 2002), 55–57.
14. Titus Marion Karlowicz, "The Architecture of the World's Columbian Exposition" (doctorate's dissertation, Northwestern University, 1965), 68.
15. Henry Van Brunt, "Architecture at the World's Columbian Exposition," *Century Magazine* 44, 1892, 88.
16. Events also covered in in Erik Larson's *The Devil in the White City*.
17. Bolotin and Laing, 55.
18. Steve Anichini, "A Super Technical Look At the Lighting of *BioShock Infinite*," *Kotaku*, March 6, 2014, http://kotaku.com/the-science-behind-bioshock-infinites-beautiful-world-1537743502.
19. Chris Remo, "Ten Things You Should Know About BioShock Infinite: Day 6," *Irrational Games Insider*, September 11, 2010, http://irrationalgames.com/insider/ten-things-you-should-know-about-*BioShock-Infinite*-day-6/.

20. Critical Path, "CRITICAL PATH-Robin Hunicke-Games Are about Choice."
21. Really Freakin' Clever, "Why Mario is more Immersive than Call of Duty," *YouTube*, February 22, 2015, https://www.youtube.com/watch?v=RUJstqS6mdE&index=59&list=WL.
22. Patricia Hernandez, "Some Don't Like BioShock's Forced Baptism. Enough To Ask For A Refund," *Kotaku*, April 16, 2013, http://kotaku.com/some-dont-like-BioShocks-forced-baptism-enough-to-as-473178476.
23. Galloway, 65.
24. Chris Remo, "Ten Things You Should Know About BioShock Infinite: Day 5," *Irrational Games Insider*, September 15, 2010, http://irrationalgames.com/insider/ten-things-you-should-know-about-BioShock-Infinite-day-5/.
25. Robert and Rosalind Lutece, "Heads or Tails," *Dialogue*, The Fairgrounds.
26. Elizabeth, *Dialogue*, Sea of Doors.

CHAPTER 5

Conclusion: There's Always a Lighthouse, a Man, and a City

Abstract The conclusion compares all three games to each other in regards to ludonarrative synchronicity, but also how this methodology is affected by analyzing each game individually versus together. It asks why ludonarrative synchronicity matters and explores the future of *BioShock* franchise.

Keywords Franchise • 2K Games • Tom Bissell • Player-driven

Earlier I mentioned that the strength of analyzing the *BioShock* trilogy in depth, rather than focusing on a group of separate, unrelated titles, was that it allowed for multiple interrelated points of comparison and correlation that appear in all three games (theme, level design, and immersion) This made it clearer to see *how* they formed (or failed to establish) the subject of player choice & control. While each game has its own degree of ludonarrative synchronous strength and weakness when evaluated individually, upon reviewal as part of the series the level of ludonarrative synchronicity per game can alter due to franchise components and hermeneutic horizons. Depending on the order players play the trilogy, there are certain expectations of what makes or breaks a *BioShock* game.

L. Reblin-Renshaw, *Ludonarrative Synchronicity in the 'BioShock' Trilogy*, https://doi.org/10.1007/978-3-030-63868-9_5

Level Design

BioShock and *BioShock 2* share a similar aesthetic in their look and feel of Rapture. Both games take advantage of the dystopia's architecture to heighten the affect of horror, using the eerie lighting effect of moving water to produce strange visuals and focus on the use of echoes off the Art Deco material to increase the tension. The main difference between *BioShock* and *BioShock 2* is that the sequel allows for an alteration in the level design by means of the narrative and the choices the player made that change it.

Columbia, in *BioShock Infinite*, is the utter antithesis of Rapture. The opening of the game does provide a visual transition from the level design of the first two games into the third by means of the architecture in the Church of Comstock, but the level design in *Infinite* does not benefit the combat in the same manner that Rapture does. All three games are challenging, but *Infinite*'s increased difficulty is partially due to its own lack of ludonarrative synchronicity. The game's narrative, at its core, is an escort mission. The level design, however, is fit for combat and not stealth. *Infinite*'s use of balanced, mirrored levels, where going left or right is irrelevant, does highlight the game's irrelevancy of choice as a theme.

Theme

Choice is a theme, though not always the primary, in all three *BioShock* titles. The use of plasmids, or vigors in the case of *Infinite*, as an alternative form of combat is a dynamic use of choice. Both *BioShock* and *BioShock 2* have the Little Sister system, with no equivalent featured in *Infinite*. However, this alteration in the third game is an example of ludonarrative synchronicity. The game is about the falsity of choice and including such a system would not be appropriate for the game's narrative and theme. *BioShock* inadvertently turns into a game where choice is irrelevant with the "Would You Kindly" twist, but where in *Infinite* this heightens ludonarrative synchronicity, for *BioShock* it weakens it. The triple-ending of *BioShock* does somewhat make up for this, allowing players intrigue-oriented choices with the Little Sisters affect the narrative. It is an example of individualism that *BioShock 2* dives into deeper.

Immersion

The clearest difference between all three games is the difference in the avatar and the player's relationship with the protagonist. In *BioShock*, Jack is the player. In *BioShock 2*, players are Subject Delta but have the option to ignore his backstory and play as they will. In *BioShock Infinite*, players are Booker and the game constantly reminds them of this. The amount of knowledge players have about their avatar's background is not cause for a break in immersion necessarily. The difference is in the amount of agency players have in controlling the avatar.

BioShock, by way of its thematic digression and plot, dismisses agency. *BioShock 2* and its thematic and narrative focus on individualism support players' sense of agency. *Infinite*'s lack of choice is reflected in players' inability to surmise what would Booker do. The game makes it clear by its well-defined characterization and use of dialogue what Booker wants, whether the player want the same thing or not.

Beyond theme, the games combat system in each of the games illuminates the differences in immersion. *BioShock* and *BioShock 2* have multiple dynamics, allowing the player to play the game as best suits their gaming style (ex. favoring melee combat, range, and/or stealth). *Infinite* pauses the game, slowing down the pace, and breaking immersion by having the player participate in a quick-time event rather than perform a complex or important task such as "save Jeremiah Fink."

Summary

BioShock was the first of its kind, a FPS that aimed to be a step above the narratively weaker games of its genre. The game did expose the weaknesses of the genre, such as the lack of player agency, but was unable to present an answer of how to create a coherent player-driven narrative.

BioShock 2 was able to learn from the mistakes of its predecessor and maintain its strengths. The sequel follows its own internal logic to a much higher degree than its two prequels. As mentioned previously, the development under a different set of leadership could have been the cause for the game's ability to alter weaknesses of the original while maintaining the strengths of *BioShock*.

Where *BioShock 2* took an hour or so to step out of the shadow of its predecessor, *Infinite* needed only minutes to set itself apart. Despite featuring the return of its creator to the franchise, *BioShock Infinite* is the least like a *BioShock* game, regarding featuring the tropes players had come to expect. *Infinite* had an entirely new cast, setting, and philosophies to explore. It eliminated multiple mechanics while changing the dynamics to those that remained. The game's diametrically new location mirrored the game's themes as the true antithesis to everything *BioShock* and *BioShock 2* stood for. These changes were not the issue regarding the lack of ludonarrative synchronicity in *BioShock Infinite*; if anything, the attempt to retain elements from the previous titles is what caused the narratology to be a mismatch with the ludology. Elements like vigors, while an effective combat tool, were given little explanation in the story for their existence and purpose in the world of Columbia outside of them being a franchise component. Without *Infinite*'s coda, the game does not warrant any of these elements left over from *BioShock* and *BioShock 2* that by being jammed in weaken the ludonarrative synchronicity.

Why Does Ludonarrative Synchronicity Matter?

The ludonarrative synchronicity of a video game is NOT a measurement of quality. A game can still be "fun," or however one wishes to define successful, even if it lacks a strong relationship between narratology and ludology. As exemplified by the success of *BioShock* and *BioShock Infinite*, ludonarrative synchronicity does NOT guarantee financial or critical success. If that was the case, then *BioShock 2* would be the "blockbuster" classic game its prequels are or were regarded as. I hypothesize that *BioShock Infinite* would not have made such a splash initially if the game was not part of the *BioShock* franchise, despite this change resulting in possibly stronger ludonarrative synchronicity. By keeping just enough franchise components like the combat system with its superhuman attacks, regardless of their lack of necessity or connection to the plot, *Infinite* was able to please fans of the previous games. *Infinite* marked the return of the franchise's creator and thus was regarded as the true sequel to *BioShock*. While *BioShock 2* featured more instances of ludonarrative synchronicity, it was not made by Levine and Irrational Games and thus seen as the stepchild of the *BioShock* series. However, it should be noted that while the praise towards *Infinite* began to diminish months after its release, *BioShock 2* has gained favor over the years.

Ludonarrative synchronicity is NOT an artistic achievement. Levine wanted to create something more than "interactive fiction," or purely objective-based.[1] For him, the debate between whether a video game should focus more on narratology or ludology was invalid. Instead of favoring one over the other, Levine wanted to have the two meet in the middle; he wanted to build the impossible. Levine is not alone in voicing the desire for more player-driven narrative video games. Tom Bissell believes it is possible, just not easy.

> The person who finally figures out how to make the game many gamers seem to believe they want—the action-heavy shooter with great characters and thoughtful scenarios—is basically going to be the Twelfth Imam of mass entertainment, and by that I mean we'll all be waiting for this figure's appearance, and his or her game, for a long, long time.[2]

Aiming for this balance is a noble artistic choice, but a developer cannot and should not expect financial and critical reciprocation for trying to achieve what some have deemed impossible. Theorists and academics will continue to debate on narratology and ludology. Critics will clamor on about how

[I]t is extremely difficult—maybe impossible—to come up with a story and characters that, when placed within the context of most current video games, ***don't*** feel inherently silly.[3]It is difficult to achieve, but more importantly, it is the market that will ultimately dictate its necessity and success in execution.

What ludonarrative synchronicity is, rather than a judge of quality, fun, or craftsmanship, a methodology to evaluate ***how*** a text functions. Ken Levine was deliberate in his intentions for the *BioShock* franchise to intertwine narratology and ludology, and therefore the connection or its absence does reveal whether the developers met their goal. If such player-driven games as Levine and Bissell desired are to be achieved, then developers need to know ***how*** previous titles have failed to reach such expectations.

Game Over?

The dream of a game, particularly a ***BioShock*** game, featuring both a narrative and gameplay centered efficiently on players' choice and control is not dead. Even with the restructuring of Irrational Games, this did not mark the end for the *BioShock* series. Irrational Games' external company, 2K Games, retained the rights to produce more titles for the franchise. It was assumed their Marin-based studio, which was the core team behind

BioShock 2, would be the site of any future *BioShock* games. In the fall of 2016, with assistance from Blind Squirrel Games, 2K Games published *BioShock: The Collection*. The remastered versions of the trilogy, despite technical flaws upon its release, proved that interest remained in the franchise and what it represents.

In 2018, it was rumored that another Marin-based company, Hangar 13 (also a subsidiary of 2K Games) would be bringing us the newest installment of *BioShock*.[4] None of this was confirmed by 2K util over a year later, when a press release in December 2019 dropped. In it 2K clarified that the newly formed studio, Cloud Chamber, would develop the next iteration in the *BioShock* franchise. According to Kelley Gilmore, the Global Studio head of Cloud Chamber:

> We founded Cloud Chamber to create yet-to-be-discovered worlds—and their stories within—that push the boundaries of what is possible in the video game medium. Our team believes in the beauty and strength of diversity, in both the makeup of the studio and the nature of its thinking. We are a deeply experienced group of game makers, including many responsible for *BioShock*'s principal creation, advancement and longstanding notoriety, and honored to be part of the 2K family as stewards of this iconic franchise.[5]

Yet-to-be discovered worlds? Will Cloud Chamber continue the trend set by *Infinite* and not return to either Rapture or Columbia? It is unclear as no other information has been released from 2K since the end of 2019. What is certain is that Ken Levine will not be involved.

Before the release of *BioShock Infinite*, Levine addressed fans directly via a blog post on the game's website:

> There are two core principles for us that define a *BioShock* game. First, it has to be set in a world that is both fantastical and yet grounded in the human experience. Second, it has to provide gamers with a large set of tools, and then set them loose in an environment that empowers them to solve problems in their own way.[6]

The *BioShock* franchise fell short of Levine's goal, but just as the character of Booker DeWitt tried and tried again, it is not out of the realm of possibility for Ken Levine, another *BioShock* team, or an intrepid group of indie developers to attempt the so-called impossible once more. According to the Lutece Twins, "One goes into an experiment knowing one could fail. But one does not undertake an experiment knowing one HAS failed."[7]

Notes

1. Grant Tavinor, "Videogames and Interactive Fiction," *Philosophy and Literature* 29, no 1 (2005): 36.
2. Tom Bissell, "Thirteen Ways of Looking at a Shooter," *Grantland,* July 12, 2012, http://grantland.com/features/line-explores-reasons-why-play-shooter-games/.
3. Ibid.
4. Alissa McAloon, "Report: 2K Games has a new *BioShock* game in the works," *Gamasutra*, April 13, 2018, https://www.gamasutra.com/view/news/316562/Report_2K_Games_has_a_new_BioShock_game_in_the_works.php.
5. "2K Announces Newly-Formed Studio – Cloud Chamber™ – Developing Next Iteration in Acclaimed BioShock® Franchise," *Business Wire*, December 09, 2019, https://www.businesswire.com/news/home/20191209005224/en/.
6. IG. Ken, "A Message from Ken Levine," *Irrational Games*, August 12, 2010, http://irrationalgames.com/insider/announcement-from-ken-levine/.
7. Robert and Rosalind Lutece, *Dialogue*, The Lighthouse.

References

"2K Announces Newly-Formed Studio – Cloud Chamber™ – Developing Next Iteration in Acclaimed BioShock® Franchise." *Business Wire*. December 09, 2019. https://www.businesswire.com/news/home/20191209005224/en/.

Aarseth, Espen. "Computer Game Studies, Year One." *Game Studies*, 1, no. 1 (July 2007), http://gamestudies.org/0101/editorial.html.

———. *Cybertext: Perspectives on Ergodic Literature*. JHU Press, 1997.

———. "Game Studies: How to Play – Ten Play-Tips for Aspiring Game-Studies Scholar." *Game Studies* 19, no. 2 (2019).

Abbott, H Porter. *The Cambridge Introduction to Narrative*. Cambridge University Press, 2008.

Ajar. "BioShock Spoiler Thread." *The Escapist* (forum). August 26, 2007. http://www.escapistmagazine.com/forums/read/9.48000-BioShock-Spoiler-Thread#318863.

Anichini, Steve. "A Super Technical Look At the Lighting of *BioShock Infinite*." *Kotaku*. March 6, 2014. http://kotaku.com/the-science-behind-bioshock-infinites-beautiful-world-1537743502.

Annander, Martin. "Boom, Headshot!" *Gamasutra*, 2017. https://gamasutra.com/blogs/MartinAnnander/20170425/296704/Boom_Headshot.php.

Barthes, Roland. *S/Z*. Translated by Richard Miller. New York: Hill and Wang, 1974.

Barton, Matt. *Dungeons & Desktops: The History of Computer Role-Playing Games*. A K Peters, Ltd., 2008.

Bayer, Patricia. *Art Deco Architecture: Design, Decoration and detail from the twenties and thirties*. London: Thames and Hudson, 1992.

L. Reblin-Renshaw, *Ludonarrative Synchronicity in the 'BioShock' Trilogy*, https://doi.org/10.1007/978-3-030-63868-9

Bissell, Tom."Vicodin Visions." *Grantland*. May 31, 2012a. http://grantland.com/features/on-rockstar-games-max-payne-3/.

———. "Thirteen Ways of Looking at a Shooter." *Grantland*. July 12, 2012b. http://grantland.com/features/line-explores-reasons-why-play-shooter-games/.

Bolotin, Normon and Christine Laing. *The World Columbian Exposition: The Chicago World's Fair of 1893*. Chicago: University of Illinois Press, 2002.

Breeze, Carla. *American Art Deco: Architecture and Regionalism*. New York: W.W. Norton & Company, 2003.

Burford, GB. "Five Things Every Great First-Person Shooter Needs." *Kotaku*, October 31, 2014. http://kotaku.com/five-things-every-great-first-person-shooter-needs-1653281844.

Burgun, Keith. "Games, Stories, and Words." *Gamasutra*, March 27, 2015, http://www.gamasutra.com/blogs/KeithBurgun/20150327/239867/Games_Stories_and_Words.php.

Carbone, Daniel. "Death and Ethical Violence." *Kotaku*. April 29, 2010. http://kotaku.com/5527216/death-and-ethical-violence.

Cifaldi, Frank. "Analysts: FPS 'Most Attractive' Genre for Publishers." *Gamasutra*. 2006. https://www.gamasutra.com/view/news/99195/Analysts_FPS_Most_Attractive_Genre_for_Publishers.php.

Cobbett, Richard. "BioShock 2 retrospective." *Eurogamer*. July 4, 2013. http://www.eurogamer.net/articles/2013-04-07-bioshock-2-retrospective.

Cobley, Paul. "Narratology." In *The John Hopkins Guide to Literary Theory & Criticism*, edited by Michael Groden, Martin Kreiswirth, and Imre Szemen, 2005. http://litguide.press.jhu.edu/.

Costikyan, Greg. "I Have No Words & I Must Design." In *The Game Design Reader: A Rules of Play Anthology*, edited by Katie Salen and Eric Zimmerman. Cambridge: The MIT Press, 2006.

Costikyan, Greg. "Where Stories End and Games Begin." *Game Developer*. September 2007.

Cowen, Nick. "BioShock 2 developer interview." *The Telegraph*, January 13, 2010. http://www.telegraph.co.uk/technology/video-games/6980675/BioShock-2-developer-interview.html.

Critical Path. "CRITICAL PATH-Robin Hunicke-Games Are about Choice." *YouTube*. March 2, 2015. https://www.youtube.com/watch?v=dhZYQbEW0nM&list=WL&index=64.

Desmond John M. and Peter Hawkes. *Adaptation: Studying Film & Literature*. New York: McGraw-Hill, 2006.

Dille, Flint and John Zuur Platten. *The Ultimate Guide to Video Game Writing and Design*. Los Angeles: Lone Eagle Publishing Company, 2007.

Egenfeldt-Nielsen, Simon, Jonas Heide Smith, and Susana Pajares Tosca. *Understanding Video Games: The Essential Introduction*. New York: Routledge, 2016.

Elise, Trihn. "Game Narrative: Thinking Outside the Lines." *Gamasutra*. February 20, 2014. http://www.gamasutra.com/blogs/EliseTrinh/20140220/206179/Game_narrative_thinking_outside_the_lines.php.

Flanagan, Mary and Helen Nissenbaum. *Values at Play in Digital Games*. Boston: MIT Press, 2014.

Franklin, Seb. *Control: Digitality as Cultural Logic*. Cambridge: MIT Press, 2015.

Frasca, Gonzalo. "Ludology Meets Narratology: Similtude and differences between (video)games and narrative." *Ludology*. 1999. http://www.ludology.org/articles/ludology.html.

Galloway, Alexander. *Gaming: Essays on Algorithmic Culture*. Minneapolis: University of Minnesota, 2006.

Genette, Gérard. *Narrative Discourse: An Essay in Method*. Translated by Jane E. Lewin. New York: Cornell UP, 1980.

Gillen, Kieron. "The New Games Journalism." *Kieron Gillen's Workblog*. May 13, 2005. http://gillen.cream.org/wordpress_html/assorted-essays/the-new-games-journalism/.

Goldberg, Harold. *All Your Bases Are Belong To Us*. New York: Three Rivers Press, 2011.

Grayson, Nathan. "Fire Away: Spec Ops, Far Cry 3 Writers on Criticizing FPS." *Rock Paper Shotgun*. April 9th 2013. https://www.rockpapershotgun.com/2013/04/09/fire-away-spec-ops-far-cry-3-writers-on-criticizing-fps/.

Graziani, Gabe. "BioShock (X360)." *GameSpy: BioShock Review*, August 16, 2007. https://web.archive.org/web/20071107015831/http://xbox360.gamespy.com/xbox-360/bioshock/813243p3.html.

Gregg, Melissa and Gregory J. Seigworth. "An Inventory of Shimmers" In *The Affect Theory Reader*, edited by Melissa Gregg and Gregory J. Seigworth, 1–27. Durham: Duke UP, 2010.

Griliopoulos, Dan. "BioShock," *XBOX 360: The Official Xbox Magazine*, August 24, 2007. https://web.archive.org/web/20071007024828/http://www.oxm.co.uk/article.php?id=1182.

Grossberg, Lawrence. *Cultural Studies in the Future Tense*. Durham: Duke UP, 2010.

Haimberg, Yotam. "Critical Literacy: Game Criticism for Game Developers." *Well Played* 2, no. 2 (2013): 21–36.

Hamilton, Kirk. "I Hope Video Gaming's Apocalypse Now Fixation Isn't Just An Excuse for Artsy Violence." *Kotaku*. June 18, 2012. http://kotaku.com/5919342/hopefully-video-gamings-apocalypse-now-fixation-isnt-just-an-excuse-for-arty-violence.

Hansson, Mikael, and Stefan Karlsson. "A Matter of Perspective: A Qualitative study of Player-presence in First-person Video Games." Thesis, Umea University, 2016.

Heller, Anne C. *Ayn Rand and the World She Made*. New York: Doubleday, 2009.

Hernandez, Patricia. "Some Don't Like BioShock's Forced Baptism. Enough To Ask For A Refund." *Kotaku*. April 16, 2013. http://kotaku.com/some-dont-like-BioShocks-forced-baptism-enough-to-as-473178476.

Hocking, Chris. "Ludonarrative Dissonance in BioShock." *Click Nothing*. October 7, 2007. http://www.clicknothing.typepad.com/click_nothing/2007/10/ludonarrative-d.html.

Hughes, Scott. "Get real: Narrative and gameplay in *The Last of US*." *Journal of Comparative Research in Anthropology and Sociology* 6, no. 1 (Summer 2015): 149–154.

Hunicke, Robert et al. "MDA: A formal approach to game design and game research," Workshop at the Game Developers Conference, San Jose, CA. 2001–2004.

IG. Ken. "A Message from Ken Levine." *Irrational Games*. August 12, 2010. http://irrationalgames.com/insider/announcement-from-ken-levine/.

IG. Admin. "From the Vault-The BioShock Pitch." *Irrational Games*. May 20, 2010. http://irrationalgames.com/insider/from-the-vault-may/.

Irrational Games' Official Channel. "Rapture: A Modern Day Atlantis?" *YouTube* October 4, 2013. https://www.youtube.com/watch?v=UsJDrsKNYxI.

Jameson, Fredric. *Signatures of the Visible*. New York: Routledge, 1992.

Jenkins, Henry. "Game Design as Narrative Architecture." In *The Game Design Reader: A Rules of Play Anthology*, edited by Katie Salen and Eric Zimmerman, 670–689. Cambridge: The MIT Press, 2006.

Karlowicz, Titus Marion. "The Architecture of the World's Columbian Exposition." Doctorate's dissertation, Northwestern University, 1965.

Kersting, Erik. "Competitive Depth and Exploitation in 'Sumer Smash Bros. Melee'." *Pop Matters*. Last modified March 4, 2014. https://www.popmatters.com/competitive-depth-and-exploitation-in-super-smash-bros-melee-2495682315.html.

Kietzmann, Ludwig. "Take-Two Q2 revenue up to $268M, BioShock 2 sales 'lower than expected'." *Endgadget*. June 8, 2010. http://www.engadget.com/2010/06/08/take-two-q2-revenue-up-to-268-million-bioshock-2-sales-low/.

LeBlanc, Matt. "Tools for Creating Dramatic Game Dynamics." In *The Game Design Reader: A Rules of Play Anthology*, edited by Katie Salen and Eric Zimmerman, 438–459. Cambridge: The MIT Press, 2006.

Levine. Ken. "From Shodan, to Big Daddy, to Elizabeth: The Evolution of AI Companions." Presentation at BAFTA, London, UK, March 11, 2013.

Lowe, David Garrard. *Art Deco New York*. New York: Watson-Guptill Publications, 2004.

Mallet, Yannis. "An Update on Assassin's Creed Unity from Yannis Mallat." *Assassin's Creed Live Updates*. November 26, 2014. http://assassinscreed.ubi.com/en-us/news/news_detail.aspx?c=tcm:154-186654-16&ct=tcm:148-76770-32.

Mateas, Michael and Andrew Stern. "Interaction and Narrative." In *The Game Design Reader: A Rules of Play Anthology*, edited by Katie Salen and Eric Zimmerman, 643–669. Cambridge: The MIT Press, 2006.

McAloon, Alissa. "Report: 2K Games has a new *BioShock* game in the works." *Gamasutra*. April 13, 2018. https://www.gamasutra.com/view/news/316562/Report_2K_Games_has_a_new_BioShock_game_in_the_works.php.

McMahan, Alison. "Immersion, Engagement, and Presence: A Method for Analyzing 3-D Video Games," in *The Video Game Theory Reader*, edited by Mark J.P. Wolf and Bernard Perron, 67–87. New York: Routledge, Taylor & Francis Group, 2003.

McWhertor, Michael. "BioShock 2 Review: In Case of Rapture." *Kotaku*. February 8, 2010. http://kotaku.com/5466745/bioshock-2-review-in-case-of-rapture.

Meer, Alec. "Wot I Think: Bioshock 2." *Rock, Paper, Shotgun*. February 8, 2010. http://www.rockpapershotgun.com/2010/02/08/wot-i-think-bioshock-2/.

Metzger, Peter. "Bioshock? You're soaking in it." *Los Angeles Times*. September 20, 2007. http://articles.latimes.com/2007/sep/20/news/wk-gamea20.

Murray, Janet H. *Hamlet on the Holodeck: The Future of Narrative in Cyberspace*. Cambridge: MIT Press, 1997.

Nardi, Bonnie A. *My Life as a Night Elf Priest: An Anthropological Account of World of Warcraft*. Ann Arbor, MI: University of Michigan Press, 2009.

Plante, Chris. "The final years of irrational games, according to those who were there." *Polygon*. March 6, 2014. http://www.polygon.com/2014/3/6/5474722/why-did-irrational-close-bioshock-infinite.

Payne, Matthew. "War Bytes: The Critique of Militainment in Spec Ops: The Line." *Critical Studies in Media Communication* 31, no. 4 (2014): 265–282.

Perry, Douglass C. "The Influence of Literature and Myth in Videogames." *IGN*. May 18, 2006. http://www.ign.com/articles/2006/05/18/the-influence-of-literature-and-myth-in-videogames.

Pointon, Collin. "BioShock's Meta-Narrative." In *BioShock and Philosophy: Irrational Game, Rational Book*, edited by Luke Cuddy. West Sussex: Wiley Blackwell, 2015.

Previously Recorded. "Sonic, The Most Overrated Game Ever?" *Red Letter Media*. July 28, 2014. http://redlettermedia.com/pre-rec-sonic-the-most-overrated-game-ever/.

Really Freakin' Clever. "Diddy Kong Racing." *YouTube*. May 16, 2013. https://www.youtube.com/watch?v=y7_u57q-ztE.

———. "Why Mario is more Immersive than Call of Duty." *YouTube*. February 22, 2015. https://www.youtube.com/watch?v=RUJstqS6mdE&index=59&list=WL.

Remo, Chris. "Ten Things You Should Know About BioShock Infinite: Day 5." *Irrational Games Insider*. September 15, 2010. http://irrationalgames.com/insider/ten-things-you-should-know-about-*BioShock-Infinite*-day-5/.

———. "Ten Things You Should Know About BioShock Infinite: Day 6." *Irrational Games Insider*. September 10, 2011. http://irrationalgames.com/insider/ten-things-you-should-know-about-*BioShock-Infinite*-day-6/.

Robinson, Martin. "Gamescom: BioShock Infinite Wins Game of Show." *IGN*. August 20, 2010. http://www.ign.com/articles/2010/08/20/gamescom-bioshock-infinite-wins-game-of-show.

Ryan, Tim. "Beginning Level Design, Part 1." *Gamasutra*. April 16, 1999. http://www.gamasutra.com/view/feature/131736/beginning_level_design_part_1.php.

Salen, Katie and Eric Zimmerman. "Games as Narrative." In *Rules of Play: Game Design Fundamentals*, edited by Katie Salen and Eric Zimmerman. Cambridge: The MIT Press, 2004.

Santayana, George. "What is Aesthetics?" *The Philosophical Review* 13, no. 3 (May 1904): 320–327.

Schiesel, Seth. "Genetics Gone Haywire and Predatory Children in an Undersea Metropolis." *The New York Times*. September 8, 2007. http://www.nytimes.com/2007/09/08/arts/television/08shoc.html.

Stanton, Rich. "BioShock Through The Looking Glass." *Rock Paper Shotgun*. November 26, 2014. http://www.rockpapershotgun.com/2014/11/26/bioshock-and-looking-glass/.

Stout, Mike. "Learning From The Masters: Level Design In *The Legend of Zelda*." *Gamasutra*. January 3, 2012. http://www.gamasutra.com/view/feature/134949/learning_from_the_masters_level_.php.

Swain, Eric. "In Defense of Ludonarrative Dissonance." *The Game Critique* (blog). August 5, 2010. http://www.thegamecritique.com/recent-posts/in-defense-of-ludonarrative-dissonance/2283/.

system1021. "Should I rescue or harvest little sisters?" *GameFAQs*. 2010. http://www.gamefaqs.com/xbox360/945380-bioshock-2/answers/165562-should-i-rescue-or-harvest-little-sisters.

Tavinor, Grant. "Videogames and Interactive Fiction." *Philosophy and Literature* 29, no. 1 (2005): 24–40.

Team Coco. "Conan O'Brien Reviews "Hitman:Absolution"-Clueless Gamer-CONAN on TBS." *YouTube*. November 14, 2012. https://www.youtube.com/watch?v=5XLrtLsGt_g.

Tosca, Susan. "Reading Resident Evil-Code Veronica X." In *Proceedings of DAC03*. Melbourne: RMIT Press, 2003.

Upton, Brian. *The Aesthetic of Play*. MIT Press, 2015.

Van Brunt, Henry. "Architecture at the World's Columbian Exposition." *Century Magazine* 44, 1892.

Vance, Brendan. "Ghosts of *BioShock*." *Brendan Vance* (blog). March 25, 2015. http://blog.brendanvance.com/2015/03/25/the-ghosts-of-bioshock/.

Vossen, Bart. "Level design for melee combat systems." *Gamasutra*. March 24, 2015. http://gamasutra.com/blogs/BartVossen/20150324/239562/Level_design_for_melee_combat_systems.php.

Wolf, Mark J. P. "Genre and the Video Game." In *The Medium of the Video Game*, edited by Mark J.P. Wolf, 113–137. Austin: University of Texas Press, 2001.

Yin-Poole, Wesley. "Levine: BioShock Infinite ending 'like nothing you've experienced in a video game before'." *Eurogamer*. December 18, 2012. http://www.eurogamer.net/articles/2012-12-18-levine-bioshock-infinite-ending-like-nothing-youve-experienced-in-a-video-game-before.

Index[1]

[1] Note: Page numbers followed by 'n' refer to notes.

L. Reblin-Renshaw, *Ludonarrative Synchronicity in the 'BioShock' Trilogy*, https://doi.org/10.1007/978-3-030-63868-9

CPSIA information can be obtained
at www.ICGtesting.com
Printed in the USA
LVHW111809010221
677999LV00004B/91

9 783030 638672